Second Reading

A Diary

by

Janis Walker

Author of

Alleluia! A Gospel Diary

Books by Janis Walker

ALLELUIA! A GOSPEL DIARY

FIRST READING: A DIARY

HALLELUJAH! A PSALM RESPONSE DIARY

SECOND READING: A DIARY

A TRIP TO GRACE

SHEPHERDS

MYSTERY!

Second Reading

A Diary

BY

Janis Walker

Pallium Press

Scripture quotations marked NRSV are from The New Revised Standard Version Bible, copyright 1989, Division of Christian Education of the National Council of Churches of Christ in the United States of America.

Scripture quotations marked KJV are from the The King James Version of the Bible.

Every effort has been made to insure accuracy of text and quotations, and any errors or omissions brought to our attention will be corrected in future editions.

SECOND PRINTING 2016

Pallium Press, P.O. Box 60910, Palo Alto, CA 94306-0910
We regret that Pallium Press cannot accept or return unsolicited manuscripts.

Check for new titles by Janis Walker at www.palliumpress.com

Pallium Press books are available at www.Amazon.com, www.BarnesandNoble.com, or at your favorite local independent bookstore.

cover photo: Terry Walker
cover design: Janis Walker

Copyright © 2016 by Janis Walker

All rights reserved. No part of this book may be reproduced, transmitted, stored in a retrieval system, or otherwise copied by any means whether electrical, mechanical, optical, or recording without the express written consent of Pallium Press, except for brief excerpts as part of reviews as permitted under the 1976 United States Copyright Act.

Printed in the United States of America.

ISBN 978-0-9826883-6-6

for

John and Marjorie, my parents

and Judy and John, my sister and brother

Acknowledgements

Thank you to Terry and Christopher and all my family and friends who encourage me to keep writing!

As with <u>Alleluia! A Gospel Diary</u>, <u>First Reading, A Diary</u>, and <u>Hallelujah! A Psalm Response Diary</u>, this book offers my personal reflections and prayers based on the daily Mass readings.

Unless otherwise indicated, the Scripture quotations are from the <u>New Revised Standard Version</u> (NRSV) of the Holy Bible.

Please read the Scripture passage slowly and prayerfully before reading the reflections and prayer.

The Second Reading is read during the Mass on Sundays and holy days.

A.M.D.G.

21 November 2015

The Presentation of the Blessed Virgin Mary

Year A

Advent 93

Christmas 96

Lent 105

Easter 114

Pentecost 120

Year B

Advent 1

Christmas 5

Lent 12

Easter 21

Pentecost 26

Year C

Advent 47

Christmas 50

Lent 56

Easter 64

Pentecost 69

Sunday, November 27, 2011 First Sunday in Advent Year B
1 Corinthians 1, 3-9
Greeting; Thanksgiving

Faithful!

God will keep us firm to the end. Not because of any merit on our part, but because of who GOD is. God is faithful and has called us into communion with his Son.

"He will also strengthen you to the end, so that you may be blameless on the day of our Lord Jesus Christ. God is faithful; by him you were called into the fellowship with his Son, Jesus Christ our Lord (vv. 8-9)."

Lord Jesus, thank you that you are my Brother and will hold my hand and lead me safely to the house of our Father. Thank you for the Holy Spirit who is helping me to learn how to be with you and how to serve you. Alleluia!

Sunday, December 4, 2011
Second Sunday in Advent
2 Peter 3, 8-14
Denial of the Parousia; Exhortation to Preparedness

Patience! Preparation for our new life requires patience.

"The Lord is not slow about his promise, as some think of slowness, but is patient with you, not wanting any to perish, but all to come to repentance (v. 9)."

Suddenly! The Lord, although very patient, will come suddenly!

"But the day of the Lord will come like a thief, and then the heavens will pass away with a loud noise, and the elements will be dissolved with fire, and the earth and everything that is done on it will be disclosed (v. 10)."

Life will change dramatically. "And the world and its desire are passing away, but those who do the will of God live forever (1 John 2, 17)."

Security? Safety? Our security is in the Lord. We are safe with the Lord.

Lord Jesus, thank you for your incredible patience with us. We have been warned that the present heavens and earth will vanish and that there will be a new earth and new heavens. Righteousness will reign because you, our true King, will reign at last. Come, Lord Jesus. Let us live in purity as we joyfully await your coming in glory. Alleluia!

Thursday, December 8, 2011
The Immaculate Conception of the Blessed Virgin Mary
Ephesians 1, 3-6, 11-12
The Father's Plan of Salvation; Inheritance through the Spirit

"Blessed be the God and Father of our Lord Jesus Christ has blessed us in Christ with every spiritual blessing in the heavenly places, just as he chose us in Christ before the foundation of the world to be holy and blameless before him in love. He destined us for adoption as his children through Jesus Christ … (vv. 3-5a)."

Chosen! Even before the beginning of the world God had already chosen us to be his daughters and sons, his own beloved children.

Chosen! God chose the Virgin Mary to be the pure Mother of his own Son.

God also chose us and predestined us through Jesus Christ. We were predestined to be his children.

For heaven's sake! Literally. Literally.

This was a mystery. Paul was granted insight into the very mystery of Christ.

Everyone knew that the Jews were God's own people, his chosen people. The "mystery" was that the Gentiles were also chosen.

Chosen to be God's children. Chosen to be full co-heirs with the Jews.

The Gentiles were not second class citizens. They were chosen to be full partners in the promise.

"There is no longer Jew or Greek, there is no longer slave or free, there is no longer male and female; for all of you are one in Christ Jesus (Galatians 3, 28)." ONE!

Paul, the Jew who had persecuted Christians, was given the assignment of telling the Gentiles about this mystery.

Paul announced the Good News to the Gentiles that God had chosen them, by adoption, to be holy and to exist for God's glory.

Lord Jesus, how can all this be? Help us this Advent to comprehend who we are, who we really are, whether or not we are Jews. We know that the Jews, your own sisters and brothers, are called God's chosen people. Help us to comprehend that God has also chosen the Gentiles to be adopted as his own children. We are your brothers and sisters, too, if we are Gentiles. Thank you that we are truly one because of what you have done for us. Let us live today for your glory. Alleluia!

Sunday, December 11, 2011 Third Sunday of Advent
1 Thessalonians 5, 16-24
Church Order; Concluding Prayer

"Rejoice always, pray without ceasing, give thanks in all circumstances, for this is the will of God in Christ Jesus for you (vv. 16-18)."

Be glad. Rejoice!

We are called to rejoice always. No matter what our circumstances are, we are to rejoice and to be glad in the LORD. The Lord is in control.

Pray! We are to pray continually.

Our whole day is a dialogue with the Lord. We need to learn to be silent and to listen to the Lord as well as to pour out our heart to him.

Thanks. Give thanks to the Lord!

No matter what our circumstances are, the Lord is with us and is in control. Giving thanks is God's will for us. When we give thanks to the Lord, we honor the Lord by our trust in him.

The Holy Spirit! We are not to quench or to grieve the Holy Spirit.

"Do not quench the Holy Spirit. Do not despise the words of prophets, but test everything; hold fast to what is good; abstain from every form of evil (vv. 19-22)."

Prophetic utterances! The words spoken by prophets. We may not recognize them or understand them right away, but we are not to despise them.

The Lord will give us understanding. We pray to the Holy Spirit to give us the gift of discernment.

Test! We are to test everything and to keep what is good.

Evil! We are to refrain from every kind of evil and even the appearance of evil.

"May the God of peace himself sanctify you entirely; and may your spirit and soul and body be kept sound and blameless at the coming of our Lord Jesus Christ. The one who calls you is faithful and he will do this (vv. 23-24)."

Lord Jesus, on this Gaudete Sunday, as we delight in seeing the rose candle on the Advent wreath and the beautiful rose vestments, let us delight even more in you! Let us learn this second half of Advent to be still, to be silent, and to expect you to come to us, to appear to us, and to transform us. Alleluia!

Sunday, December 18, 2011 Fourth Sunday of Advent
Romans 16, 25-27
Doxology

"Now to God who is able to strengthen you ... to the only wise God, through Jesus Christ, to whom be the glory forever! Amen (vv. 25a, 27)."

Strength! It is GOD who alone can strengthen us to complete the course he has assigned to us. To GOD alone be the glory for what is accomplished in us and through us.

"The LORD will fulfill his purpose for me... (Psalm 138, 8). This is a promise!

My part is to trust the Lord, to obey the Lord, and to follow as the Lord leads. It is ultimately up to the Lord to fulfill his plan and purpose for my life.

Lord Jesus, thank you for the Holy Spirit who strengthens us and encourages us when we grow weary and dispirited. We place all our trust in you and give you all the glory. Alleluia!

JANIS WALKER   SECOND READING

Sunday, December 25, 2011   The Nativity of the Lord
Titus 2, 11-14
Transformation of Life

Grace! God's grace has appeared.

God's grace is available to all. God offers salvation to all. God's grace is here to train us to live for God.

Lord Jesus, thank you for giving yourself for us to redeem us and to purify us. Thank you for the joy and confidence you give us as we choose to live for you and await your coming in glory. Alleluia!

Friday, December 30, 2011   The Holy Family
Colossians 3, 12-21
Renunciation of Vice; The Christian Family

Location. Location. Location. Where in the world are we?

Earlier in this chapter of Colossians (Colossians 3, 1-3), we are told where we are, as Christians. We have been raised with Christ and we are already, in one sense, in the heavenly realm.

Therefore, as we live here on earth, we are to seek that which is "above," where our true life is and where our Lord Jesus Christ is, at the right hand of God, our Father. Our "real" life is a hidden life. It is hidden with Christ in God. We are to think and to concentrate on the heavenly realm.

Although our "real" life is above, where Christ is, we still live here on earth until we are called to our true home. My Scottish neighbor, Elizabeth, who lived to be 102, used to say that we have to wait for "the invitation."

Dress code! There is a certain dress code we are to observe. This is how to dress for true success.

We are to put off thoughts and behavior unbecoming to a Christian. We are to " … get rid of … anger, wrath, malice, slander and abusive language … (Colossians 3, 8)." "Do not lie to one another, seeing that you have stripped off the old self with its practices and have clothed yourselves with the new self, which is being renewed in knowledge, according to the image of its creator (Colossians 3, 9, 10)."

We are to put on our true self. We are to be dressed in gentleness, compassion, humility, and patience. The most important "vestment" is that of LOVE.

We are to be enveloped in love. We are to be clothed in love. We are to be controlled by the peace of God. I have learned, if I do not have peace about something, not to do it.

How does this translate to family life? In one word, humility!

"As God's chosen ones, holy and beloved, clothe yourselves with compassion, kindness, humility, meekness, and patience. Bear with one another and, if anyone has a complaint against another, forgive each other; just as the Lord has forgiven you, so you must also forgive. Above all, clothe yourselves with love, which binds everything together in perfect harmony (vv. 12-14). Wives are to be subordinate to their husbands. Husbands are to love their wives. Children are to be obedient to their parents. Parents are cautioned not to provoke or to discourage their children. "And let the peace of Christ rule in your hearts …(v. 15a)."

Lord Jesus, thank you for the Holy Spirit who reminds us who we are, where we are, and how we are to dress. Alleluia!

Sunday, January 1, 2012 Mary, Mother of God
Galatians 4, 4-7
God's Free Children in Christ

Time! " … when the fullness of time had come, God sent his Son, born of a woman, born under the law, in order to redeem those who were under the law, so that we might receive adoption as children (vv. 4-5)."

Time! It's time!

I remember those words, spoken by my nurse in the labor room, as I was taken into the delivery room at Stanford Hospital to give birth to Christopher.

Labor had gone on forever, it seemed, but the big moment was here at last! It was time!

Time! When the time was ripe and full, God sent his own Son to live with us. It was God's idea to adopt us.

Through faith and baptism, we are Jesus' sisters and brothers. God is our Father. "… in Christ Jesus you are all children of God through faith. As many of you were baptized into Christ have clothed yourselves with Christ (Galatians 3, 26, 27)."

Abba! God the Father sent the Holy Spirit of Jesus, his Son, into our hearts to cry out "Abba, Father."

Lord Jesus, how wonderful this is! We are your brothers and sisters. Rejoicing, we hold up our faces and our hearts up to our loving Abba, Father. Alleluia!

Sunday, January 8, 2012 The Epiphany of the Lord
Ephesians 3, 2-3, 5-6
Commission to Preach God's Plan

It's for you! Whatever God has given me is meant for you.

And, guess what! Whatever God has given you is for me.

St. Paul understood this. He knew that the grace God had given to him, a Jew, was meant to be shared with the Gentiles.

The Gentiles were not to be considered second-string or second-class Christians. The Gentile Christians were co-heirs with the Jewish Christians.

The esteemed Sulpician Scripture scholar, Fr. Raymond Brown, understood this. It is said that Fr. Brown even recommended reading the book of Ephesians every day.

You count. You're IN! I count. I'm IN.

We are in the Body of Christ. We are members of the Body of Christ on earth, the Church. We don't need to compete with one another.

Lord Jesus, whether or not we are Jewish by ethnicity, you call us and you welcome us into relationship with you. Let us go out into the world to live the Gospel and to proclaim the Gospel. Your grace is available to us all. Alleluia!

Sunday, January 15, 2012 Second Sunday in Ordinary Time
1 Corinthians 6, 13-15, 17-20
Sexual Immorality

Do you know that " ... your body is a temple of the Holy Spirit within you, which you have from God, and that you are not your own? For you were bought with a price; therefore glorify God in your body

(vv. 19, 20)."

Know whose you are! You belong to the Lord. I belong to the Lord.

Our bodies are members of Christ. We are one spirit with the Lord.

Lord Jesus, I want to live freely and forever for you and for your purpose in my life. Prune from me any thoughts, words, or actions that are not in keeping with your plan for me. Let me never grieve the gentle Holy Spirit. Let me honor you in every aspect of my life as you lead me to the house of our Father. Alleluia!

Sunday, January 22, 2012 Third Sunday in Ordinary Time
1 Corinthians 7, 29-33
Advice to Virgins and Widows

Time! St. Paul cautioned the Christians in Corinth, a Greek city known for its immorality, that time was short. He warned that " ... the appointed time has grown short ... (v. 29a.)."

Time is also short for us, no matter how much time we have left to live in this world. The world as we know it will not be here forever.

"And the world and its desire are passing away, but those who do the will of God live forever (1 John 2, 17)."

Lord Jesus, we turn to you and place all our temporal concerns into your hands. Thank you for your sovereignty over all our relationships. Thank you for the Holy Spirit who teaches us how to live to glorify you and to be ready when you call us to the house of our Father. Alleluia!

Sunday, January 29, 2012 Fourth Sunday of Ordinary Time
1 Corinthians 7, 32-35
Advice to Virgins and Widows

Free or anxious? Believing that Jesus would return very soon, Paul was advising the Corinthians to live in such a way as to be free to serve the Lord wholeheartedly.

Not all the apostles were single. Peter was married.

In the contemporary Roman Catholic Church, there are married priests who were formerly ordained, usually as Episcopalians or Anglicans. This is called the Pastoral Provision of Pope Saint John Paul II.

Lord Jesus, thank you that the Holy Spirit is here to teach us to follow you and to love and serve others according to your will for our lives. Alleluia!

Thursday, February 2, 2012 The Presentation of the Lord
Hebrews 2, 14-18
Exaltation through Abasement

Priest! Jesus is our merciful Priest as well as our Brother. He understands us perfectly. He is completely faithful to us.

Jesus knows what it is like to be human. He is fully human and fully divine. He knows what it is like to suffer. He knows what is like to be tested and tried through suffering. He knows.

"Because he himself was tested by what he suffered, he is able to help those who are being tested (Hebrews 2, 18)."

Jesus knows we are still afraid of death. Yes, we loudly profess the resurrection of our Lord and Savior Jesus Christ, but we are still in some trepidation about death. At least I am.

Jesus, our priest, is interceding for us, for you and for me. One day, he will hold out his hand and say, "Come to Me." We will be Home at last, in the house of our Father.

Lord Jesus, thank you that you have destroyed the power of death. Death did not win. YOU won! Thank you for the freedom to live for you with joy and confidence. Alleluia!

Sunday, February 5, 2012 Fifth Sunday in Ordinary Time
I Corinthians 9, 16-19, 22-23
Reason for Not Using His Rights; All Things to All

Paul was constrained to preach the Gospel! "If I proclaim the gospel, this gives me no ground for boasting, for an obligation is laid on me, and woe to me if I do not proclaim the gospel (v. 16)!"

Paul reminds me of Jeremiah, the suffering prophet, who lamented, "If I say, 'I will not mention him, or speak any more in his name,' then within me there is something like a burning fire shut up in my bones; I am weary of holding it in, and I cannot (Jeremiah 20, 9)."

Paul knew very well that he could have claimed the privileges of the other apostles. "This is my defense to those who would examine me. Do we not have the right to our food and drink? Do we not have the right to be accompanied by a believing wife, as do the other apostles and the brothers of the Lord and Cephas [Peter]? Or is it only Barnabas and I who have no right to refrain from working for a living? Nevertheless, we have not made use of this right, but we endure anything rather then put an obstacle in the way of the gospel of Christ (I Corinthians 9, 3-6, 12b)."

Although Paul was free, he willingly chose to be a slave to all in order to win as many as possible to Christ. He did everything for the sake of the Gospel.

Lord Jesus, thank you for all the blessings you have poured upon us to sustain us as we seek to serve you. You understand all our tears and trials. Thank you for the freedom we have to offer ourselves to you freely. We belong completely to you and you will care for us. Thank you for calling us to live the Gospel and to proclaim the Gospel. Alleluia!

Sunday, February 12, 2012   Sixth Sunday in Ordinary Time
1 Corinthians 10, 31 - 11, 1
Seek the Good of Others

Seek! When we seek to please ourselves, we become driven. We are always trying to make sure we have our own way. We may become addicted to having our own way.

Seek! When we seek to please the Lord, our focus changes. Gradually. The Lord is very gentle with us. Gradually we learn to seek the Lord in each situation.

Seek! Whether we are eating, drinking, or whatever we are doing, we are seeking to do everything for the glory of GOD! We are seeking to live for the benefit of others.

Lord Jesus, thank you for transforming our hearts to desire to glorify you and to live for the good of others. Alleluia!

Sunday, February 19, 2012 Seventh Sunday in Ordinary Time
2 Corinthians 1, 18-22
Paul's Sincerity and Constancy

YES! In Jesus, " … it is always 'Yes.' For in him every one of God's promises is a 'Yes. (v. 19b, 20a).' "

YES! Whatever our outer question, God's answer to us is "yes." God knows what it is we truly are seeking.

God's answer to some of the things we are asking for is a firm "no." God knows what is best for us. God's answer is always "yes" to us, however, to the deepest longings of our restless hearts.

God accepts us, loves us and cares for us. God knows how to open and to close doors for us. God truly knows what is best for us.

The gift of the Holy Spirit in our hearts is the first installment, or the guarantee, of what God will accomplish in us and through us.

We are sealed with the Holy Spirit. We are anointed. We are marked. We belong to God.

Lord Jesus, thank you that you are faithful to us and you are answering "yes" to the deepest desires you have planted in our hearts. Alleluia!

Wednesday, February 22, 2012 Ash Wednesday
2 Corinthians 5, 20 - 6, 2
The Ministry of Reconciliation; The Experience of the Ministry

God " … reconciled us to himself through Christ, and has given us the ministry of reconciliation; that is, in Christ God was reconciling the world to himself, not counting their trespasses against them, and entrusting the message of reconciliation to us. So we are ambassadors for Christ, since God is making his appeal through us; we entreat you on behalf of Christ, be reconciled to God. For our sake he made him to be sin who knew no sin, so that in him we might become the righteousness of God (2 Corinthians 5, 18-20)."

Ambassadors! Because of God's action in reconciling us to himself in Christ, we are charged with a mission. We are ambassadors for our Lord Jesus Christ. We now pray and work for others to be reconciled to God.

For us and for our salvation, God the Father actually made his beloved Son, Jesus, to become sin, to BE sin, in order that we would be considered righteous. This is the grace of God exploding upon us, within us, and through us.

Lord Jesus, even though we cannot comprehend this gift all at once, we thank you for your total surrender, on our behalf, into the hands of God, your Father, your Daddy, your Abba. How could you do that? How could you love us so much? During these beautiful days of springtime, this Lent, let us learn more and more what our salvation means. Thank you for holding our hand and leading us through this Lent.

Sunday, February 26, 2012 First Sunday of Lent
1 Peter 3, 18-22
Christian Suffering

Suffering! We just don't want to go there.

Jesus, the sinless one, suffered. He suffered for us. Jesus suffered for our sins, so we could go free.

Mysteriously, after Jesus died and was brought to life in the Spirit, he took a trip. Where on earth did he go?

Actually he didn't go anywhere on earth at that time. He went to another place.

He went to preach to the imprisoned spirits of those who had disobeyed God and had not been saved during the flood. Only eight people were saved by boarding Noah's ark.

Salvation! St. Peter tells us that we are saved through baptism.

"And baptism ... now saves you – not as a removal of dirt from the body, but as an appeal to God for a good conscience, through the resurrection of Jesus Christ, who has gone into heaven and is at the right hand of God, with angels, authorities, and powers made subject to him (vv. 21-22)."

St. Paul tells us that "when you were buried with him in baptism, you were also raised with him through faith in the power of God, who raised him from the dead (Colossians 2, 12)."

As St. Paul also tells us, "Do you not know that all of us who have been baptized into Christ Jesus were baptized into his death? Therefore we have been buried with him by baptism into death, so that, just as Christ was raised from the dead by the glory of the Father, so we too might walk in newness of life. For if we have been united with him in a death like his, we will certainly be united with him in a resurrection like his (Romans 6, 3-5)."

Heaven! Jesus, the one who suffered for us, is now the Risen Lord who is in heaven with God and the holy angels. This helps to put all suffering into perspective.

Lord Jesus, when we suffer for doing good, let us offer our suffering to you. You know how to transform all our suffering and to use it for your purposes. Thank that all that is now hidden from our understanding shall one day be bright. Thank you for the waters of our baptism and the new life you offer us.

Sunday, March 4, 2012 Second Sunday of Lent
Romans 8, 31-34
God's Indomitable Love in Christ

"If God is for us, who is against us? He who did not withhold his own Son, but gave him up for all of us, will he not with him also give us everything else (vv. 31b-32)?"

Our spirits soar when we know, deep within, that God is for us! No one can stop God's loving plan for us from being fulfilled.

Lord Jesus, thank you that you are interceding for us at the right hand of our Father. You became human like us and you know exactly how to pray for us. You know exactly what we need. Thank you for reassuring us that you love us and you are caring for us. Thank you for setting us free to follow you all the way Home.

Sunday, March 11, 2012 Third Sunday of Lent
1 Corinthians 1, 22-25
Paradox of the Cross

No "slanting!" The apostle Paul refused to slant his preaching to either the Jews or the Greeks.

He straight out proclaimed the crucified Christ to all! It is to all that Christ is the power of God. It is to all that Christ is the wisdom of God.

Sometimes, as Christians, we are tempted to slant our witness. If we go to a certain prayer group and do not carry the translation of the Bible that is usually read there, we may hedge our bets and carry the translation "they" seem to prefer and to pray the way "they" pray.

We cannot afford to play these games. Only the Holy Spirit can guide us to proclaim Christ as we are called.

Lord Jesus, thank you for strengthening us to proclaim you in all your power and in all your wisdom. Let us be true to ourselves by being true to you.

Sunday, March 18, 2012 Fourth Sunday of Lent (Laetare Sunday)
Ephesians 2, 4-10
Generosity of God's Plan

First, the bad news. "You were dead through trespasses and sins in which you once lived, following the course of this world …. All of us once lived … in the passions of our flesh, following the desires of flesh and senses … (Ephesians 2, 1-3)."

Now, the good news. God is greater than our sins!

God, who is " … rich in mercy, out of the great love with which he loved us even when we were dead through our trespasses, made us alive together with Christ – by grace you have been saved – and raised us up with him and seated us with him in the heavenly places with Christ Jesus …. For by grace you have been saved through faith, and this is not your own doing; it is the gift of God – not the result of works, so that no one may boast (vv. 4-6, 8,9)."

We have been saved by grace through faith. Even the faith, or the trust, operative in our salvation is God's gift. It is not a result of what we have done, our "works," but it is God's amazing gift.

We are now free to serve God as we are called to serve. God has all sorts of good works already prepared for us.

Lord Jesus, it is almost impossible for us to wrap our minds around this gift of grace, so freely given. You gave your very life for us. You have made it possible for us to follow you and to do the work you have assigned to us. We place all our trust in you as we offer ourselves for your service. Praise to you, Lord Jesus Christ!

Monday, March 19, 2012 St. Joseph
Romans 4, 13, 16-18, 22
Inheritance through Faith

Stay the course! We are in a race and we can't just faint and get off the track.

Abraham really had to stay the course. He had to wait a long, long, long time for the fulfillment of God's promise. It seem beyond impossible for the promise of God to come to pass.

God is the only one who " … gives life to the dead and calls into being what does not exist. He [Abraham] believed, hoping against hope … (vv. 17-18)."

Our power to stay the course must come from God. Abraham " … did not doubt God's promise in unbelief; rather, he was empowered by faith and gave glory to God and was fully convinced that what he had promised he was also able to do (Romans 4, 20-21).

Lord Jesus, I am exhausted. How can I stay the course? Help me to trust you.

Sunday, March 25, 2012 Fifth Sunday of Lent
Hebrews 5, 7-9
Jesus, Compassionate High Priest

Jesus understands us. He understands our suffering.

"In the days when he was in the flesh, he offered prayers and supplications with loud cries and tears to the one who was able to save him from death, and he was heard because of his reverence. Son though he was, he learned obedience from what he suffered …
(Hebrews 5, 7-9)."

This is a hard passage. It is also a very comforting passage.

The <u>King James Version</u> of the Bible even says that Jesus " … offered up prayers and supplications with strong crying and tears unto him that was able to save him from death …. (Hebrews 5, 7 KJV)."

Jesus, our compassionate priest, knew what it was to pray and to weep. Still, he was always reverent. He was always obedient to his Father, his beloved Abba.

Jesus told his disciples, " … My food is to do the will of him who sent me and to complete his work (John 4, 34)."

When we love and respect someone a great deal, we hold them in profound reverence. We shrink from doing anything that would dishonor them because we love them so much.

Lord Jesus, if you had to learn obedience through what you suffered, how much more do we need to learn obedience through what we suffer. We don't like to suffer! It hurts. Thank you for your presence with us in our suffering. Help us to honor you with our trust, our reverence, and our obedience.

Monday, March 26, 2012 The Annunciation of the Lord
Hebrews 10, 4-10
One Sacrifice instead of Many

Jesus came into the world to carry out the plan of God. He came to do the will of his Father, no matter what the cost.

The cost was his own blood. He is the Lamb of God who shed his precious blood and took away our sins.

"And it is by God's will that we have been sanctified through the offering of the body of Jesus Christ once for all (v. 10)."

Lord Jesus, thank you that your once for all sacrifice is made present to us at Mass. We proclaim your death and your resurrection until you come again.

Sunday, April 1, 2012 Palm Sunday of the Lord's Passion
Philippians 2, 6-11
Plea for Unity and Humility

Kenosis! Emptying. Relinquishing.

Jesus knew who he was, Son of God, and yet he did not come to earth to assert his divinity. He came to earth to live out, to the full, his humanity as Son of Man.

As the words of a hymn by James Montgomery so eloquently remind us, "When Jesus left his Father's throne, he chose an humble birth; like us, unhonored and unknown, he came to dwell on earth."

As our brother, he came to show us how to live in constant contact, as he did, with our Father in heaven. Over and over, Jesus told us that he only did what his Father had instructed him to do.

His humility and his obedience led him to the Cross. Only at the Cross could he complete the Father's mission on our behalf.

Jesus took us with him to the Cross! As St. Paul proclaimed, " … I have been crucified with Christ; and it is no longer I who live, but it is Christ who lives in me. And the life I now live in the flesh I live by faith in the Son of God, who loved me and gave himself for me (Galatians 2, 19b-20)."

When Christ died, WE died! Our sins died. Jesus, the Lamb of God, took them away.

First, the Cross. Now, the Crown!

"Therefore God also highly exalted him and gave him the name that is above every name, so that, at the name of Jesus every knee should bend, in heaven and on earth and under the earth, and every tongue should confess that Jesus Christ is Lord, to the glory of God the Father (vv. 9-11)."

God exalted his Son with the name above all names. At Jesus' name, all will kneel and proclaim that Jesus is Lord.

Lord Jesus, as we enter Holy Week, we offer ourselves to you. Cleanse us and remove from us anything that does not honor and glorify you. Forgive us for all the ways in which we have injured ourselves and injured others. Help us to be compassionate with ourselves as well as with others. Thank you for the Holy Spirit who will lead us through this week with you.

> Thursday, April 5, 2012 Holy Thursday
> 1 Corinthians 11, 23-26
> The Lord's Supper; Tradition of the Institution

"For I received from the Lord what I also handed on to you, that the Lord Jesus on the night when he was betrayed took a loaf of bread, and when he had given thanks, he broke it and said, 'This is my body that is for you. Do this in remembrance of me.' In the same way he took the cup also, after supper, saying, 'This cup is the new covenant in my blood. Do this, as often as you drink it, in remembrance of me.' For as often as you eat this bread and drink the cup, you proclaim the Lord's death until he comes (1 Corinthians 11, 23-26)."

From the LORD! The tradition of the Lord's Supper was not just some idea of St. Paul.

This tradition was from the Lord Jesus Christ! Paul was merely handing on to the Christians in Corinth what he himself had received from the Lord.

Proclaim! We not only eat the Body of Christ and drink the Blood of Christ, but we also announce or proclaim his death until he comes again in glory.

In <u>The Roman Missal</u> (2011), in one of the concluding rites, the deacon or priest says, "Go and announce the Gospel of the Lord."

Lord Jesus, let us truly announce the Gospel by the way we live. Thank you for leading us gently through this Holy Week. Thank you for giving us your very self in Holy Communion.

> Friday, April 6, 2012 Good Friday
> Hebrews 4, 14-16, 5, 7-9
> Jesus, Compassionate High Priest

Jesus, our High Priest, understands us completely. He sympathizes with us in all our struggles. He understands our tears and our frustration.

He knows. He knows exactly what we are going through at this very moment.

He also knows that we will not be stuck here, in this difficulty, forever. He is leading us through to a new place of trust, a new place of joy.

Confidence! We are invited to approach the very throne of God with confidence that we may receive the mercy and the grace that will set us free to live.

"For here we have no lasting city, but we are looking for the city that is to come. Through him [Jesus], then, let us continually offer a sacrifice of praise to God ... (Hebrews 13, 14-15a)." The majestic hymn "O God Beyond All Praising," (Thaxted) exhorts us to offer our sacrifice of praise to God.

Lord Jesus, you were no stranger to suffering. Even you were required to learn obedience through suffering. Let us be brave and run to you and pour out our broken and crushed hearts to you, knowing that you will heal us. You shed your Blood for this very purpose. We love you and relinquish ourselves into your hands.

Saturday, April 7, 2012 Holy Saturday/ Easter Vigil
Genesis 22, 1-18
The Testing of Abraham

"Ready!" When God called his servant Abraham, Abraham answered by saying, "Here I am," or "Ready."

Ready? How could Abraham possibly have said that if he really knew what lay ahead?

Altar! Years and years before, Abraham, who was already elderly, had placed his hopes, his dashed hopes, for a son, on the altar, figuratively speaking.

"Hoping against hope, he believed that he would become 'the father of many nations,' according to what was said, 'So numerous shall your descendants be.' He did not weaken in faith when he considered his own body, which was already as good as dead (for he was about a hundred years old), or when he considered the barrenness of Sarah's womb. No distrust made him waver concerning the promise of God, but he grew strong in his faith as he gave glory to God, being fully convinced that God was able to do what he had promised (Romans 4, 18-22)."

Altar!

Now, it appeared that God was requiring that Abraham literally place Isaac, his beloved son, the answer to his prayers, on the altar. How could God ask this?

Trust!

Abraham was not blinded by fear. Instead he was seeing with the eyes of trust. After all, he had had a long time to learn to trust, really to trust God, for the impossible.

Abraham even said to his servants, "Stay here ... the boy and I will go over there; we will worship, and then we will come back (v. 5)." Notice he said "WE!"

Abraham was convinced that God would provide. "God himself will provide the lamb... (v. 8)." And, indeed Abraham and Isaac both returned alive and well.

To honor Abraham's radical trust and obedience, the Lord poured out countless blessings on him. "I will indeed bless you, and I will make your offspring as numerous as the stars of heaven and as the sand that is on the seashore ... because you have obeyed my voice (vv. 16b-18)."

Lord Jesus, ready or not, we are here to lay on the altar all that you have promised us. We place all our trust in you. ALLELUIA!

Sunday, April 8, 2012
Easter Sunday of the Resurrection of the Lord
Colossians 3, 1-4
Mystical Death and Resurrection

Above! "So if you have been raised with Christ, seek the things that are above, where Christ is, seated at the right hand of God ... for you have died and your life is hidden with Christ in God. When Christ, who is your life is revealed, then you also will be revealed with him in glory (vv. 1, 3, 4)."

Our real life is with Christ in the heavenly realm. Our real life, even now, is a hidden life with the Lord Jesus Christ.

Our life here on earth is temporary. When Christ returns in glory, our real life, our true life, will also appear.

Lord Jesus, thank you for reminding us that our life here on earth is temporary. We live for you and follow you while we are still on earth, but the best is yet to come, when you return in glory. ALLELUIA!

Sunday, April 15, 2012 Second Sunday of Easter
Divine Mercy Sunday
1 John 5, 1-6
Faith is Victory over the World

Earlier this week, I ran into an old friend whom we last saw a year or so ago. Although he is a Christian, he is still full of bitterness and hatred for Christians who injured him years ago. He can speak of nothing else.

Time alone does not heal. Only God can bring healing.

This letter from John tells us clearly that if we love the Father we also love those who are begotten by this same Father. We don't have to pretend that they are good or that they haven't hurt us.

Our love for God is manifested by our obedience. "By this we know that we love the children of God, when we love God and obey his commandments. For the love of God is this, that we obey his commandments (vv. 2, 3a)."

At the Last Supper, Jesus told his disciples, "I give you a new commandment, that you love one another. Just as I have loved you, you also should love one another. By this everyone will know that you are my disciples, if you have love for one another (John 13, 34-35)."

Victory! The Lord wants us to live in victory. The victory that conquers and overcomes all the evil in this world is our faith, our trust in the Lord's victory.

Lord Jesus, you came through both water and blood. You lived and died and rose again so that we could live in your Easter victory. Thank you for your great mercy poured out upon us to forgive our sins. Thank you for freeing us and for giving us your own mercy with which to forgive those who have injured us. Thank you for your gift or peace, your Easter peace. ALLELUIA!

Sunday, April 22, 2012 Third Sunday of Easter
1 John 2, 1-5
Christ and His Commandments

Advocate and intercessor! Jesus is my advocate and my intercessor.

He knows me through and through. He understands the motivation for my thoughts, my words, and my actions.

Jesus is the expiation, the perfect offering, for my sins. He has atoned for my sins.

He is the perfect offering for your sins. He is the perfect offering for the sins of everyone in the whole wide world. He is the Lamb of God who takes away our sins.

How do we know that we know Jesus? Do we have to have some kind of feeling?

No, not according to the Scriptures. It is clearly written that we know him if we keep his commandments (vv. 3-6). When we obey him, God's love is being perfected in us.

Lord Jesus, thank you that you are my advocate and my intercessor. I don't have to defend myself. Thank you for the Holy Spirit who reminds me that you are watching over me and watching out for me. Let me honor you with my trust and my love which is manifested in my obedience to you. ALLELUIA!

Sunday, April 29, 2012 Fourth Sunday of Easter
1 John 3, 1-2
Children of God

"See what love the Father has given us, that we should be called children of God; and that is what we are. The reason the world does not know us is that it did not know him. Beloved, we are God's children now; what we shall be has not yet been revealed. What we do know is this: when he is revealed, we will be like him, for we will see him as he is. (1 John 3, 1-2)."

Child! Children!

On the receiver of our wall phone in the kitchen, there is a little sticker which says "Child of God." When I see it, I am reminded that I am a child of God speaking to another child of God.

So what if the "world" doesn't know or doesn't care about us? The "world" did not know God even when God paid a visit in person, in the Person of his Son, Jesus. Jesus was the stone rejected which became the very cornerstone.

Now! We are already God's dear children right now. What we shall become has yet to be fully revealed. How exciting!

Lord Jesus, thank you that when we see you as you are, we shall be like you. You are our Good Shepherd. As we live in this glorious hope, let us honor you by following you with love and trust. Let us live with purity, expectancy, and integrity. ALLELUIA!

Sunday, May 6, 2012 Fifth Sunday of Easter
1 John 3, 18-24
Avoiding Sin; Confidence before God

"Little children, let us love, not in word or speech, but in truth and action (v. 18)." In other words, we are not just to talk about love, but our actions are express our love.

Greater! God is greater than our hearts, greater than our feelings. God knows everything.

God knows how to confront us when we need to acknowledge our sins, confess our sins, and then repent of our sins. The truth is hard, but it sets us free.

God commands us not only to believe in the name of Jesus, his Son, but also to love one another. "All who hate a brother or sister are murderers, and you know that murderers do not have eternal life abiding in them (1John 3, 15)."

We remain in God as we keep his commandments. The Holy Spirit empowers us to keep his commandments.

Lord Jesus, thank you for the Holy Spirit who confronts us, comforts us, and strengthens us to keep our Father's commands. Thank you for abiding in us and for reassuring us that we abide in you. ALLELUIA!

Sunday, May 13, 2012 Sixth Sunday of Easter
1 John 4, 7-10
God's Love and Christian Life

"She doesn't know God!" I still remember that profound observation from Christopher when he was five years old.

Alas, he was referring to a very troubled teacher in a public school. As Christopher explained, "She's unhappy because she doesn't know God."

"Beloved, let us love one another, because love is from God; everyone who loves is born of God and knows God (v. 7)." St. John tells us that a person without love does not really know God, because God is love. God literally pours his love into our hearts (Romans 5, 5).

Life! God the Father sent Jesus, his Son, to us in order that we might have life, true life, through him

Love! It's not that we loved God first. It's that God loved us first and sent Jesus as the payment for our sins.

Lord Jesus, thank you for loving us first. You loved us before we even thought of you. You came as our Friend and you gave your life for us. Thank you for the Holy Spirit who shines through us today, revealing your love for others. ALLELUIA!

Sunday, May 20, 2012 The Ascension of the Lord
Ephesians 1, 17-23
The Church as Christ's Body

"God mounts his throne to shouts of joy; a blare of trumpets for the Lord." The responsorial psalm for today, Psalm 47, is pulsing with joy and with victory.

Head! Christ is the Head of his Church.

Head! The Church is the Body of Christ and Christ is the Head.

Lord Jesus, on this "blare of trumpets" day, this day when we celebrate your return, mission gloriously accomplished, to your Father in heaven, let us remember that we are truly your Body here on earth. You are our Head. Let us live and love as you call us. ALLELUIA!

Sunday, May 27, 2012 Pentecost Sunday
1 Corinthians 12, 3-7, 12-13
Unity and Variety; One Body, Many Parts

GOD! Father, Son, and Holy Spirit.

Gifts! The Holy Spirit gives gifts that differ.

The Holy Spirit is the same. The gifts are different. There are many different ways of serving the Lord.

"For just as the body is one and has many members, and all the members of the body, though many, are one body, so it is with Christ. For in the one Spirit we were all baptized into one body – Jews or Greeks, slaves or free – and we were made to drink of one Spirit. Now you are the body of Christ and individually members of it (vv. 12-13, 27)."

Lord Jesus, thank you that you are the Head of your Body, the Church, and that we are members of your Body. Thank you for the gifts the Holy Spirit has poured out upon us in order to serve you. Let us rejoice in you, glorify you, and serve you in the Church as you have called us to serve. ALLELUIA!

Sunday, June 3, 2012 The Most Holy Trinity
Romans 8, 14-17
Children of God through Adoption

"For all who are led by the Spirit of God are children of God. For you did not receive a spirit of slavery to fall back into fear, but you have received a spirit of adoption. When we cry 'Abba! Father!' it is that very Spirit bearing witness with our spirit that we are children of God … (vv. 14-16)."

Out! We need to get out of living in fear.

How do we learn not to live in fear? We learn to live in reality.

The reality is wonderful! The reality is that God has reached out tenderly to us and has adopted us.

It is TRUE! We belong to God.

We are free to live as God's own beloved daughters and sons because that is who we really are. The Holy Spirit lives within us and reminds us of our true identity.

We are heirs! We are unbelievably wealthy. We are heirs of Christ.

Our suffering with Christ leads to our being glorified with Christ. Christ is Victor!

Lord Jesus, thank you for the Holy Spirit who reminds us that we are your brothers and sisters and that God is our Father. Today, let us step out, maybe for the first time, and dare to live with the confidence you died and rose again to give us. Alleluia!

> Sunday, June 10, 2012 Corpus Christi
> The Most Holy Body and Blood of Christ
> Hebrews 9, 11-15
> Sacrifice of Jesus

"But when Christ came as a high priest of the good things that have come, then … he entered once for all into the Holy Place, not with the blood of goats and calves, but with his own blood, thus obtaining eternal redemption (vv. 11-12)."

Once! Christ entered once into the celestial sanctuary. He won our redemption with his own blood, not with the blood of sacrificial animals. The redemption he won for us is eternal.

Clean! The blood of our Lord Jesus Christ cleanses us. We can stop doing what is useless and to begin to worship GOD, the eternal and living God.

Mediator! Jesus Christ is the mediator of the new covenant. We are invited to receive the inheritance he died to give us.

Lord Jesus, thank you that you are our Great High Priest. You are the Lamb of God who shed your blood and died for us to live. You are the Bread of Life. We worship you and pray that our lives will glorify you. Alleluia!

> Friday, June 15, 2012 The Most Sacred Heart of Jesus
> Ephesians 3, 8-12, 14-19
> Commission to Preach God's Plan; Prayer for the Readers

Paul, who once persecuted Christians, never forgot the grace of God operating in his life. He marveled at the generosity of God's grace which was given to him to proclaim the Gospel to the previously despised and scorned Gentiles.

The Gentiles were actually co-heirs, full members of the Body of Christ, the Church. They were not second class citizens. They were not "second string."

The Church! The wisdom of God is meant to be manifested through the CHURCH (vv. 8-10). This is " ... the church of the living God, the pillar and bulwark of the truth (1 Timothy 3, 15b)."

It is through the Body of Christ, the Church, that " ... the wisdom of God in its rich variety might now be known to the rulers and authorities in the heavenly places (v. 10)."

Paul knelt before his heavenly Father to pray for the Christians in Ephesus and for us. He prayed that the Holy Spirit living within us would strengthen us to comprehend the love of the Lord Jesus Christ. This love surpasses, far surpasses, all the knowledge in the world.

Lord Jesus, thank you that the Holy Spirit who dwells within us is teaching us each day more and more of your love for us. Thank for the grace given to us to comprehend these mysteries. Alleluia!

Sunday, June 17, 2012   Eleventh Sunday in Ordinary Time
2 Corinthians 5, 6-11
Our Future Destiny

Aspirants! We are all aspirants as we follow the Lord. We are aspiring to please the Lord. That is our goal.

Courageous! We are called to follow the Lord in gutsy faith, trusting the Lord to lead us to the place he has prepared for us.

Lord Jesus, thank you for the Holy Spirit who gives us courage each day to follow you all the way Home. Let us rejoice that we will one day stand before you, look into your eyes, and worship you throughout all eternity. Alleluia!

Saturday, June 23. 2012   Vigil of the Nativity of John the Baptist
1 Peter 1, 8-12
Blessing

For you! For you! For you!

The prophets long, long ago, were prophesying about God's grace for YOU! They were serving you by prophesying about the salvation won for you by the Lord Jesus Christ. The Holy Spirit was telling them how to express the Gospel to you.

You and I have not seen Christ, yet we believe in him. We manifest our love for him by our obedience to him (John 14, 15).

Lord Jesus, we rejoice as we consider the goal of our faith which is the salvation of our souls. Thank you for the sufferings you endured in order to secure our salvation. Angels longed to see into what you have freely given to us. We rejoice in you and thank you for all the prophets who have been sent to us. Alleluia!

Sunday, June 24, 2012 The Nativity of John the Baptist
Acts 13, 22-26
Paul's Address in the Synagogue

Context! It was in the synagogue of Antioch, that Paul recounted salvation history (vv. 16-21).

David! God removed Saul from being king and chose David to be king.

God knows how to do this. "For not from the east or from the west and not from the wilderness comes lifting up; but it is God who executes judgment, putting down one and lifting up another (Psalm 75, 6-7)."

David, the king after God's own heart, was the one who carried out God's every wish. From King David's descendants, God chose to bring forth Jesus.

Herald! John the Baptist, after his long preparation in the desert, knew his identity and his vocation. He was the herald who proclaimed to Israel a baptism of repentance. He knew that he was not worthy to untie the sandals of Jesus, who would come after him.

Lord Jesus, let us carry out your every wish and complete our course. Let us be heralds of your coming in glory. Alleluia!

Sunday, July 1, 2012 Thirteenth Sunday in Ordinary Time
2 Corinthians 8, 7, 9, 13-15
Generosity in Giving

Money. "The money talk!"

I remember after a special Mass at the seminary some years ago, the young priest who had been the presider turned to the seminary president and inquired, "Is it time for the money talk?!

The key in giving is found in 2 Corinthians 8, 5. We give ourselves first to the Lord and then to the work the Lord has for us to do.

Jesus is our example. Rich though he was, he became poor for us. He became poor so that we could become rich in the true sense.

Again, I was reminded of the beautiful hymn which begins, "When Jesus left his Father's throne, he chose an humble birth; like us, unhonored and unknown, he came to dwell on earth." The hymn is by James Montgomery and the music is "Kingsfold," an English folk melody.

Lord Jesus, thank you that you came to bring us to life, true life, abundant life. Life to the full! Thank you for the Holy Spirit who touches our hearts and our bank accounts to share with others. Let us learn to be gracious receivers as well as givers. Alleluia!

Sunday, July 8, 2012 Fourteenth Sunday in Ordinary Time
2 Corinthians 12, 7-10
Paul's Boast: His Weakness

Incorporation! Paul decided to include, or to incorporate his "thorn" into his ministry.

At first, quite naturally, he just wanted to get rid of the "thorn." Three times he beseeched the Lord to remove the "thorn." The Lord said no.

Content! At last Paul learned to be content in this difficult situation

He was learning that the Lord's grace was sufficient for him to live, even with this "thorn" in his life. He knew he needed the power of Christ even more in order to continue his ministry.

He knew that when he realized his weakness, the Lord was there to strengthen him. "Therefore I am content with weaknesses, insults, hardships, persecutions, and calamities for the sake of Christ; for whenever I am weak, then I am strong (v. 10)."

Lord Jesus, it is really hard to serve you with these irritating "thorns." We need you! Thank you for filling us with your love and your strength to continue to serve you. Let us honor you by our trust that you are in control. Alleluia!

Sunday, July 15, 2012 Fifteenth Sunday in Ordinary Time
Ephesians 1, 3-14
The Father's Plan of Salvation
Fulfillment through Christ, Inheritance through the Spirit

"Blessed be the God and Father of our Lord Jesus Christ, who hath blessed us with all spiritual blessings in heavenly places in Christ (v. 3 KJV)."

Chosen! Chosen for holiness.

Destined! Destined for adoption!

Before the foundation of the world, God our Father chose us to be holy. This is made possible by Jesus, God's own beloved Son, who shed his blood for our redemption.

Free! We are now free and will spend the rest of our time on earth learning to understand and to live in this exhilarating freedom.

The Holy Spirit. The Holy Spirit is the guarantee or the first "installment" of the inheritance which has been lavished upon us.

This is bigger that we think! We are drawn by Love into the very mystery of the will of God, the daring plan of God to sum up EVERYTHING in Christ!

Lord Jesus, thank you that we are sealed and marked as your own forever. Thank you for leading us deeper and deeper into the wonders of our Father's plan for us. Thank you for the Holy Spirit who reminds us who we are, God's own beloved children. Alleluia!

Sunday, July 22, 2012 Sixteenth Sunday in Ordinary Time
Ephesians 2, 13-18
One in Christ

Outside! Everyone, at one time or another, has felt like an outsider looking in.

Inside! Jesus has made it possible for us to be on the inside, right in the heart of his family.

St. Paul, who was Jewish and once persecuted Christians, was chosen by God to tell non-Jews that they were also included in the Church, the very Body of Christ on earth.

No more walls! Jesus, by shedding his Blood on the Cross, smashed down all the walls that have divided us.

"He has abolished the law with its commandments and ordinances, that he might create in himself one new humanity in place of the two, thus making peace, and might reconcile both groups to God in one body through the cross … (vv. 15-16)."

Jesus! It is through Jesus that we have access in the Holy Spirit to our Father in heaven.

Lord Jesus, we marvel at what you have done for us. Let us live this day honoring you by serving our sisters and brothers. Alleluia!

Sunday, July 29, 2012 Seventeenth Sunday in Ordinary Time
Ephesians 4, 1-6
Unity in the Body

Worthy! St. Paul is entreating us to live in a manner worthy of our vocation.

Earlier this week, I just blew up and acted in a manner most unworthy of the call to follow Christ. Forgive me, Lord.

Humility. Gentleness. Patience. Lovingly putting up with each other. Sincerely striving for unity. All these wonderful qualities are part and parcel of our call.

One. One. One. One.

There is one Lord. There is one faith. There is one baptism. There is one God and Father of us all.

Lord Jesus, thank you for the Holy Spirit who empowers us to live out our call to follow you. No matter how discouraged we become with ourselves and with others, you are lovingly leading us each day closer and closer to the house of our Father. Home. Alleluia!

Sunday, August 5, 2012 Eighteenth Sunday in Ordinary Time
Ephesians 4, 17, 20-24
Renewal in Christ

How do we live? Living cynically with a sense of futility is not how we are called to live. That is not how Christ teaches us to live.

Change clothes! We are to "take off" the way we formerly lived.

We are invited to allow the Holy Spirit to renew our way of thinking and to clothe us in our new self, our real self, created in truth and righteousness.

"I will greatly rejoice in the LORD, my whole being shall exult in my God; for he has clothed me with the garments of salvation, he has covered me with the robe of righteousness, as a bridegroom decks himself with a garland, and as a bride adorns herself with her jewels (Isaiah 61, 10)."

Lord Jesus, than you that you have made it gloriously possible for us to be clothed in YOU! Let us step out, with confidence, to live this day in our new attire, our new life in you. Alleluia!

Monday, August 6, 2012 The Transfiguration of the Lord
2 Peter 1, 16-19
Apostolic Witness

Peter, James, and John actually saw Jesus dazzlingly transfigured before their very eyes! The Father in heaven again confirmed his identity. "This is my Son, my Beloved, with whom I am well pleased (v. 17)."

Lord Jesus, when we fall into late summer doldrums, thank you for reviving us. We are revived when we remember who YOU are! You are God's beloved Son. You are our Brother. Let the morning star rise in our hearts as we behold your shining presence. Alleluia!

Sunday, August 12, 2012 Nineteenth Sunday in Ordinary Time
Ephesians 4, 30 - 5, 2
Rules for the New Life

"Therefore be imitators of God, as beloved children, and live in love, as Christ loved us and gave himself up for us, a fragrant offering and sacrifice to God (5, 1)."

We are entreated not to grieve the Holy Spirit. It is with the Holy Spirit that we have been sealed for our redemption.

It is the Holy Spirit who gives us the power to live as God calls us to live, in love. We are not only to be in love, but also to live in love.

Lord Jesus, thank you that you will do what we cannot do by ourselves. Thank you for sending the Holy Spirit to remove all bitterness from our hearts. Thank you for the Holy Spirit who teaches us to love and forgive others as you love and forgive us. Alleluia!

Wednesday, August 15, 2012
The Assumption of the Blessed Virgin Mary
1 Corinthians 15, 20-27
Christ the Firstfruits

"If Christ has not been raised, your faith is futile and you are still in your sins. Then those also who have died in Christ have perished. If for this life only we have hoped in Christ, we are of all people most to be pitied. But in fact Christ has been raised from the dead, the firstfruits of those who have died. For since death came through a human being, the resurrection of the dead has also come through a human being; for as all die in Adam, so all will be made alive in Christ 9 (1 Corinthians 15, 17-22)."

This will all happen in God's time and in God's order. Christ is first, the firstfruits, " … then at his coming those who belong to Christ. Then comes the end when he hands over the kingdom to God the Father, after he has destroyed every ruler and every authority and power. For he must reign until he has put all his enemies under his feet (vv. 23-25)."

What is the last enemy? Death.

Death was not God's idea. In this passage, death is referred to as an enemy, as the last enemy. "The last enemy to be destroyed is death (v. 26)."

Lord Jesus, you willingly submitted yourself to the plan of your Father. You live, died, rose again, and will return in glory so that God will truly be all in all. Let us joyfully anticipate your return as we live today to do your will. Alleluia!

Sunday, August 19, 2012 Twentieth Sunday in Ordinary Time
Ephesians 5, 15-20
Duty to Live in the Light

Watch! We're accustomed to watching others and to watching out for others.

Watch! St. Paul cautions us to watch OURSELVES and how we live.

Wise. We are to be wise because we are living in evil times. Remember, Jesus told his followers to be as wise as serpents and yet as innocent as doves (Matthew 10, 16).

Will! The will of God. The will of God is our sanctification (1 Thessalonians 4, 3)."Do not be conformed to this world, but be transformed by the renewing of your minds, so that you may discern what is the will of God – what is good and acceptable and perfect (Romans 12, 2)." We are praying to understand God's will for us.

Wine! We are not to become drunk on wine, but rather to be filled with the Holy Spirit as we offer our thanks to God. A book by Fr. Rainero Cantalessa, O.F.M., <u>Sober Intoxication of the Holy Spirit</u>, offers wonderful insights on how the Holy Spirit brings us true joy.

Lord Jesus, thank you for the Holy Spirit who teaches us how to live with others and how to praise you. Alleluia!

Sunday, August 26, 2012 Twenty-first Sunday in Ordinary Time
Ephesians 5, 21-32
Wives and Husbands

A mutual respect and admiration society! We are reminded to " ... live in love, as Christ loved us and gave himself up for us, a fragrant offering and sacrifice to God (Ephesians 5, 2)."

St. Paul acknowledges that he is dealing with a mystery. "This is a great mystery, and I am applying it to Christ and the church (v. 32)."

CHRIST! It is Christ who is our reference point. "Be subject to one another out of reverence for Christ (v. 21)."

As to the Lord. Wives are to be subject to their husbands as to the Lord.

Sacrificial love. Husbands are to love their wives with the same sacrificial love with which Christ loves the Church.

The husband who truly loves his wife truly loves himself (v. 28). He nourishes and cherishes himself and is called to nourish and cherish his wife. His wife is called to respect her husband.

Lord Jesus, thank you for the Holy Spirit who teaches us how to love and respect you and how to love and respect one another in the mysterious sacrament of holy matrimony. Alleluia!

Sunday, September 2, 2012
Twenty-second Sunday in Ordinary Time
James 1, 17-18, 21b-22, 27
Temptation; Doers of the Word

The word! God gave us birth by the word of truth.

The word! We joyfully welcome the God's word planted in us. God's word is able to save us and to bring us to wholeness.

The word! We are called to be doers of the word and not merely passive listeners to the word.

We are to put God's word into practice! We are to keep ourselves pure and unstained as we live in the world. We are, in particular to care for widows and orphans.

Lord Jesus, let us glorify you by our silence, by our words, both written and spoken, and by our lives of service to the afflicted and the voiceless. Alleluia!

Sunday, September 9, 2012
Twenty-third Sunday in Ordinary Time
James 2, 1-5
Sin of Partiality

Level! There is a hymn called "The Ground is Level at the Foot of the Cross."

We are reminded in today's second reading not to show partiality as we live out our faith in Christ. We are to love and to serve all, knowing that God chose the poor to be wealthy in faith and to be heirs of his kingdom.

"My brothers and sisters, do you with your acts of favoritism really believe in our glorious Lord Jesus Christ (v. 1)?"

Lord Jesus, sometimes we do show favor to some people we think are "important." Sometimes we ignore the ones who we think don't "count." Have mercy on us. Forgive us. Thank you for the Holy Spirit who pierces our hearts to show us our need of you. Thank you for the Holy Spirit who enlarges our hearts to love and to honor all. Alleluia!

Friday, September 14, 2012 The Exaltation of the Holy Cross
Philippians 2, 6-11
Plea for Unity and Humility

"Lift High the Cross!" This majestic hymn exhorts us to proclaim Christ's love to all.

"Do nothing from selfish ambition or conceit, but in humility regard others as better than yourselves. Let each of you look not to your own interests, but to the interests of others. Let the same mind be in you that was in Christ Jesus (vv. 3-5).

We have the mind of Christ (1 Corinthians 2, 16). We are also to have the same attitude as Christ.

He was and is GOD! Still, he did not seek to promote himself. He knew who he was.

Instead, Jesus poured himself out and freely took the form of a slave. He was and is GOD! Still, he stooped to become human like us and to serve us.

"And being found in human form, he humbled himself and became obedient to the point of death – even death on a cross. Therefore God also highly exalted him and gave him the name that is above every name, so that at the name of Jesus every knee should bend, in heaven and on earth and under the earth, and every tongue should confess that Jesus Christ is Lord, to the glory of God the Father (vv. 7b-11)."

Lord Jesus, we gasp at these verses. We become silent, filled with wonder and awe. We wonder how, with all our weaknesses, we can have your mind and your attitude. Thank you for the Holy Spirit who patiently teaches us how to think as you think and how to have the same attitude you have. Alleluia!

Sunday, September 16, 2012
Twenty-fourth Sunday in Ordinary Time
James 2, 14-18
Faith and Works

I love children's book illustrations! A whole story can be told without words, simply by looking at the pictures

So it is with faith and works. Does my life illustrate my faith? Or is my faith all words and no actions which illustrate my faith?

Lord Jesus, thank you for the Holy Spirit who teaches us how to live so that our lives illustrate and demonstrate our faith in you. Alleluia!

Sunday, September 23, 2012
Twenty-fifth Sunday in Ordinary Time
James 3, 16 - 4, 3
True Wisdom; Causes of Division

Sounds like bad politics! James says that where there is ambition which is merely selfish and where there is jealousy, there will result disorder and even evil.

Above! "But the wisdom from above is first pure, then peaceable, gentle, willing to yield, full of mercy and good fruits, without a trace of partiality or hypocrisy. And a harvest of righteousness is sown in peace for those who make peace (vv. 17-18)."

Lord Jesus, we pray for the Holy Spirit to purify our hearts and our motives as we seek to serve you and to serve others. Alleluia!

Sunday, September 30, 2012
Twenty-sixth Sunday in Ordinary Time
James 5, 1-6
Warning to the Rich

Weep! Wail! Wealthy. Wages. Workers.

James really goes after the unscrupulous wealthy. He confronts them, no doubt about it.

"Your riches have rotted, and your clothes are moth-eaten. Your gold and silver have rusted, and their rust will be evidence against you, and it will eat your flesh like fire (vv. 2-3a). WHEW!

He assures them that the cries of their ill-treated employees have reached heaven. The Lord always hears the cries of the poor.

Lord Jesus, thank you for the Holy Spirit who strengthens us to persevere in trusting you in the midst of injustice. Thank you that you will return in glory as our King. Alleluia!

Sunday, October 7, 2012
Twenty-seventh Sunday in Ordinary Time
Hebrews 2, 9-11
Exhortation to Faithfulness

Jesus became like US in order to be our faithful high priest, full of mercy (Hebrews 2, 17). We are, in turn, called to be conformed to the image of our Lord Jesus Christ (Romans 8, 29),

Jesus is not only our Brother but he is also our leader, our pioneer, "the captain of our salvation (Hebrews 2, 10 KJV)" and our forerunner. He truly "ran" ahead of us and led us to salvation through his suffering

Lord Jesus, thank you that you yielded to your Father and suffered on our behalf. Thank you for the Holy Spirit who sanctifies us and strengthens us to live for your glory. Alleluia!

Sunday, October 14, 2012
Twenty-eighth Sunday in Ordinary Time
Hebrews 4, 12-13
The Sabbath Rest

Rest! When we enter into God's rest, we are resting from our own works. The writer, after exhorting us to enter this rest, then instructs us about the power of God's word.

Alive! God's word is alive and effective.

"Indeed, the word of God is living and active, sharper than any two-edged sword, piercing until it divides soul from spirit, joints from marrow; it is able to judge the thoughts and intentions of the heart. And before him, no creature is hidden, but all are naked and laid bare to the eyes of the one to whom we must render an account (vv. 12-13)."

Lord Jesus, thank you that you see into the mysterious working of my heart. You know why I think and feel the way I do. You call me to cease my restless struggle, learn to settle down, and to enter into true Sabbath rest. Thank you that you are my great high priest. It is to you that I must render an account of my life. Strengthen me and purify me to think your thoughts and to live according to your plan for me. Thank you for your word which is at work in me preparing me to stand before you. Alleluia!

Sunday, October 21, 2012
Twenty-ninth Sunday in Ordinary Time
Hebrews 4, 14-16
Jesus, Compassionate High Priest

Confidently! We are called to approach God with confidence because of Jesus, our priest.

Jesus! He is our merciful and compassionate great high priest. He is our Brother who is here to intercede for us and to help us.

Lord Jesus, sometimes I get so discouraged with my failures that I almost lose hope. Thank you that you are my priest and you understand me and love me. Thank you for calling me to come to you, to pour out my heart to you, and to receive your comfort and your forgiveness. Thank you that you are very close to me in the sacrament of reconciliation and you are there to set me free. Thank you for holding my hand and for instilling new confidence in me to continue to follow you all the way Home. Alleluia!

Sunday, October 28, 2012 Thirtieth Sunday in Ordinary Time
Hebrews 5, 1-6
Jesus, Compassionate High Priest

"Every high priest chosen from among mortals is put in charge of things pertaining to God on their behalf, to offer gifts and sacrifices for sins. And one does not presume to take this honor, but takes it only when called by God, just as Aaron was (vv. 1, 4)."

Jesus! Jesus, our great high priest, is our representative before God.

Jesus is very patient with us. He knows what is like to be human like us.

One does not call oneself to be a priest. God calls. God equips.

Jesus, however, is different. Jesus is a priest forever (Hebrews 5, 6, Psalm 110, Hebrews 7, 17-21).

Lord Jesus, thank you that you do indeed understand our human weakness. You know how to lead us from where we are in our understanding of you into a deeper, fuller comprehension of you and of your priesthood. Thank you for your constant intercession for us. Alleluia!

Thursday, November 1, 2012 All Saints
1 John 3, 1-3
Children of God

"See what love the Father has given us, that we should be called children of God; and that is what we are (v. 1a)."

Now! Right now. We are God's beloved children.

We don't have to prove ourselves or perform perfectly. We are safe and secure in our identity as God's children.

Even as we joyfully sing "For All the Saints," we don't really know yet what we shall become.

"Beloved, we are God's children now; what we will be has not yet been revealed. What we do know is this: when he is revealed, we will be like him, for we will see him as he is. And all who have this hope in him purify themselves, just as he is pure (vv. 2-3)."

We do know that we are called to be conformed to the image of Christ (Romans 8, 29).

Hope! Because of this amazing hope for our future we are confident in this present time.

We do not crave to be understood, much less accepted, in our culture. "The reason the world does not know us is that it did not know him [Jesus] v. 1b)."

Lord Jesus, we yield joyfully to the work of the Holy Spirit to purify us and to prepare us for our awesome, mysterious destiny. Alleluia!

Friday, November 2, 2012 All Souls
Romans 5, 5-11
Faith, Hope, and Love

Jesus strode in and took over! We were guilty, no doubt about if, and yet we were completely helpless to remedy our situation.

In his inaugural homily on April 24, 2005, in St. Peter's in Rome, Pope Benedict XVI, spoke of Jesus as our Good Shepherd as he explained the significance of the white woolen pallium, worn over the shoulders, as the first symbol of papal ministry.

According to Pope Benedict XVI, "The symbolism of the pallium is even more concrete: the lamb's wool is meant to represent the lost, sick or weak sheep which the shepherd places on his shoulders and carries to the waters of life. For the Fathers of the Church, the parable of the lost sheep which the shepherd seeks in the desert, was an image of the mystery of Christ and the Church. The human race – every one of us – is the sheep lost in the desert, which no longer knows the way. The Son of God will not let this happen; he cannot abandon humanity in so wretched a condition. He leaps to his feet and abandons the glory of heaven, in order to go in search of the sheep and pursue it all the way to the Cross. He takes it upon his shoulders and carries our humanity; he carries us all – he is the good shepherd who lays down his life for the sheep."

We were sinners and yet unable to rescue ourselves. Jesus knew what to do. He died for us and freed us to live for him.

"But God proves his love for us in that while we were still sinners Christ died for us (v. 8)."

Jesus shed his Blood for us on the Cross and justified us by his Blood. Do you remember the hymn written by Robert Lowry, "Nothing but the Blood of Jesus?"

"For if while we were enemies, we were reconciled to God through the death of his Son, much more surely, having been reconciled, will we be saved by his life (v. 10)." Free! We are free to live for Jesus.

Lord Jesus, how can we ever thank you for cleansing us from all that defiles us and for reconciling us to God our Father? Let us never cease to marvel and to praise you for all you have done for us. Thank you for the Holy Spirit who strengthens us to live now in the light of your Cross and glorious resurrection. Alleluia!

Sunday, November 4, 2012 Thirty-first Sunday in Ordinary Time
Hebrews 7, 23-28
Melchizedek, a Type of Christ

Forever! Jesus is our forever priest. He is forever offering intercession for us

As the writer to the Hebrews tells us, " … he holds his priesthood permanently, because he continues forever. Consequently he is able for all time to save those who approach God through him, since he always lives to make intercession for them (vv. 24, 25).

Jesus, our priest, was himself was the sacrifice offered on the altar, the altar of the Cross. In the glorious Easter hymn, "At the Lamb's High Feast We Sing," Jesus is referred to as both victim and priest.

Jesus himself, holy and human, understands us and knows how to intercede for us. Jesus knows how to lead us safely to the house of our Father.

Lord Jesus, thank you for your expert intercession for us. You know us through and through and you know exactly how to pray for us. Thank you for the Holy Spirit who teaches us to be still, to listen to you, and then to do what you call us to do. Alleluia!

Friday, November 9, 2012
The Dedication of the Lateran Basilica in Rome
1 Corinthians 3. 9-11, 16-17
The Role of God's Ministers

Colleagues. Garden. Building

St. Paul reminds us that we are actually God's colleagues, God's co-workers. We are also God's garden. We are God's building.

St. Paul knew his part. He was called to lay the foundation. Another would build on this foundation.

What is the foundation? The question is actually, "WHO is the foundation?"

You know the answer. The foundation is our Lord Jesus Christ.

Temple! We are God's temple. God's Holy Spirit dwells in us.

"Do you not know that you are God's temple and that God's Spirit dwells in you? If anyone destroys God's temple, God will destroy that person. For God's temple is holy, and you are that temple (vv. 16, 17)."

Lord Jesus, how amazing this is! We are actually your colleagues. We are truly your garden, your building, your holy temple. Thank you for the Holy Spirit who teaches us how to follow you all the way to the house of our Father in heaven. Alleluia!

JANIS WALKER SECOND READING

Sunday, November 11, 2012
Thirty-second Sunday in Ordinary Time
Hebrews 9, 24-28
Sacrifice of Jesus

Heaven! When Jesus, our high priest, offered himself as sacrifice for our sins he did not enter into a temporal sanctuary. He entered into HEAVEN and appeared before God, our Father, on our behalf.

The sacrifice our Lord Jesus Christ made for us was a once for all sacrifice on the Cross. Just as we will one day die and then be judged, so Jesus was offered once to take away our sins.

The second time Jesus comes will not be to take away our sins, but to bring us into the fullness of our salvation. How eagerly we await his return!

Lord Jesus, thank you for entering into heaven itself to appear before our Father on our behalf. Thank you for the Holy Spirit who teaches us how to live for you as we await your return in glory. Alleluia!

Sunday, November 18. 2012
Thirty-third Sunday in Ordinary Time
Hebrews 10, 11-14, 18
One Sacrifice Instead of Many

ONE sacrifice! Instead of offering sacrifices over and over, Jesus offered ONE sacrifice for sin. He offered HIMSELF.

Jesus, our high priest, offered himself as our Lamb of sacrifice. He was the Lamb of God who took away the sins of the world.

Only Jesus could do this. Only Jesus, Son of Man, human like us, was also Son of God, divine like his Father in heaven.

There is no longer any need of offering sacrifices for sins. "Where there is forgiveness of these [sins], there is no longer any offering for sin (v. 18)."

Our sacrifice is one of praise. "Through him [Jesus], then, let us continually offer a sacrifice of praise to God, that is, the fruit of lips that confess his name (Hebrews 13, 15)."

What now? Jesus, seated at the right of his Father, the place of highest honor, is waiting.

Jesus is waiting until all who have made themselves his enemies become his footstool. As he waits, he actively makes intercession for us.

Lord Jesus, thank you for being our Lamb of sacrifice and for taking away our sins. Thank you that we are being consecrated by your offering of yourself on our behalf. Thank you for the Holy Spirit who is teaching us how to live for you and follow you all the way to the house of our Father. Alleluia!

Thursday, November 22, 2012 Thanksgiving
1 Corinthians 1, 3-9
Greeting; Thanksgiving

The grace of God has been lavishly bestowed on us IN Jesus Christ. In Jesus Christ we have been enriched in all ways. We are not lacking in spiritual gifts as we await the return of our King.

Lord Jesus, we get so weary, depleted, and discouraged. Thank you that you will keep us firm and steadfast to the end of our pilgrimage Home. Thank you that God our Father has called us and summoned us to be in close communion with you. We thank you and we rejoice in you! Alleluia!

Sunday, November 25, 2012
Our Lord Jesus Christ King of the Universe
Revelation 1, 5-8
Greeting

"John to the seven churches that are in Asia: grace to you and peace from him who is and who was and who is to come, and from the seven spirits who are before his throne, and from Jesus Christ, the faithful witness, the firstborn of the dead, and the ruler of the kings of the earth.

To him who loves us and freed us from our sins by his blood, and made us to be a kingdom, priests serving his God and Father, to him be glory and dominion forever and ever. Amen.

Look! He is coming with the clouds; every one will see him, even those who pierced him; and on his account all the tribes of the earth will wail. So it is to be. Amen.

'I am the Alpha and the Omega.' says the Lord God, who is and who was and who is to come, the Almighty. (Revelation 1, 8)."

Lord Jesus, thank you for strengthening us to witness faithfully to you until you return in glory. ALLELUIA!

Sunday, December 2, 2012
First Sunday of Advent   Year C
1 Thessalonians 3, 12-4,2
Concluding Thanksgiving; General Exhortations

"And may the Lord make you increase and abound in love for one another and for all, just as we abound in love for you. And may he so strengthen your hearts in holiness that you may be blameless before our God and Father at the coming of our Lord Jesus with all his saints (vv. 12-13)."

Love! We are called to increase in love and to abound in love.

Holiness! We pray to the Lord to strengthen our hearts to be holy and without blame at the coming of Jesus with his saints.

Lord Jesus, thank you for this holy time of Advent in which we may truly grow in love for you and for others. Still us to welcome silence even as the world around us rushes. Thank you for the Holy Spirit who teaches us how to live as we prepare for your coming in glory. Alleluia!

Saturday, December 8, 2012   The Immaculate Conception
Ephesians 1, 3-6, 11-12
Greeting; The Father's Plan of Salvation;
Inheritance through the Spirit

Blessed! Chosen! Destined!

God blessed us and chose us to be holy. God destined us for adoption.

We belong to God. We are not accidents.

In Christ! It is in Christ that we are blessed. It is in Christ that we are chosen. It is in Christ that we are destined for adoption.

"In Christ we have also obtained an inheritance, having been destined according to the purpose of him who accomplishes all things according to his counsel and will, so that who were the first to set our hope on Christ, might live for the praise of his glory (vv. 11-12)."

Lord Jesus, let us learn to be still this Advent and to rest in the knowledge that we are indeed blessed, chosen, and destined to live as your sisters and brothers. Your Father is our Father. Thank you for the Holy Spirit who teaches us to see ourselves as we really are, God's beloved children. Alleluia!

Sunday, December 9, 2012 Second Sunday of Advent
Philippians 1, 4-6, 8-11
Thanksgiving

With joy! Following St. Paul's example, we are invited not only to "pray," in some generic sense, but to pray with intentional JOY.

The Christians in Philippi had been faithful partners with Paul in the proclamation of the Gospel. Paul reassured them that God would complete the work God had begun in them.

"I am confident of this, that the one who began a good work among you will bring it to completion by the day of Jesus Christ (v. 6.)."

Lord Jesus, thank you for helping us this Advent to learn how to pray with joy, regardless of our circumstances. Thank you that our Father will complete the work he has begun in us. Thank you for the Holy Spirit who is helping us to discern what is of true value. Thank you for purifying us this Advent and for filling us with your righteousness and with joy. Alleluia!

Sunday, December 16, 2012 Third Sunday of Advent
Philippians 4, 4-7
Joy and Peace

Rejoice! Whatever our circumstances, we are to rejoice in the LORD. Rejoice.

Lord Jesus, thank you that you are near. Let us pour out our hearts to you. You understand us completely and you are ready to help us. Thank you for giving us your peace which strengthens us and guards our minds and our hearts. Alleluia!

Sunday, December 23, 2012 Fourth Sunday of Advent
Hebrews 10, 5-10
One Sacrifice instead of Many

A priest, in the time of Jesus, stood daily in the Temple. The priest offered sacrifices that could not truly take away sins (Hebrews 10, 11).

Jesus! Jesus was different.

Jesus came into the world to do the will of his Father in heaven. "See, I have come to do your will (v 9a)." He came to carry out the plan of his Father for our salvation.

By the will of God and according to the merciful plan of God, we are made holy. We are consecrated through the perfect offering of the Blood of our Lord Jesus Christ.

Lord Jesus, we become silent and we marvel! You, our Great High Priest, are the Lamb of God. You came to carry out your Father's plan for us. Thank you for the Holy Spirit who breathes new strength into us to continue to trust you and to follow you. Alleluia!

Tuesday, December 25, 2012 The Nativity of the Lord
Titus 2, 11-14
Transformation of Life

He's here! God's grace has burst forth upon us in the Person of an Infant.

Jesus! Jesus is here.

When Jesus appears on the scene, everything changes. The words "hopeless" and "impossible" have been removed from the dictionary of our hearts.

New! Jesus is here to write a new script for our lives.

Lord Jesus, thank you for coming from the Father in heaven to be with us. Thank you for your Blessed Mother Mary who accepted her "impossible" role in your life and therefore, in our lives. Thank you for the Holy Spirit who teaches us how to live as we joyfully anticipate your return in glory. ALLELUIA!

Sunday, December 30, 2012
The Holy Family of Jesus, Mary, and Joseph
1 John 3, 1-2, 21-24
Children of God; Confidence before God

"See what love the Father has given us, that we should be called children of God; and that is what we are. The reason the world does not know us is that it did not know him. Beloved, we are God's children now; what we will be has not yet been revealed. What we do know is this: when it is revealed, we will be like him, for we will see him as he is. And all who have this hope purify themselves, just as he is pure. Beloved, if our hearts do not condemn us, we have boldness before God; and we receive from him whatever we ask, because we obey his commandments and do what pleases him. And this is his commandment, that we should believe in the name of his Son Jesus Christ and love one another, just as he has commanded us. All who obey his commandments abide in him, and he abides in them. And by this we know that he abides in us, by the Spirit he has given us."

BELIEVE! God's command is to believe, to trust, in his beloved Son, Jesus.

After the feeding of the five thousand, Jesus told the people, "This is the work of God, that you believe in him whom he has sent (John 6, 29)."

LOVE! God also commands us to love one another.

We may not always agree with others, but we trust the Lord and pray for the Lord to bless them.

REMAIN! When we keep God's commands, we truly remain in God.

God remains in us. The Holy Spirit reassures us that this is true. We are entwined in the very life of the Holy Trinity.

Lord Jesus, thank you that we are truly God's beloved children. We don't have to be so insecure and to seek and even to crave the approval of others in a desperate, grasping way. We are safe and secure in GOD'S care. We are now free to reach out to others with care and compassion. Thank you for the big surprise ahead when our future identity will be revealed to all. Thank you for revealing to us how the Father in heaven loves us. Thank you that we may come with confidence to you and ask you to forgive all our sins and to make us pure. Thank you for forgiving our sins and inviting us to continue our pilgrimage with joy and confidence. Alleluia!

Tuesday, January 1, 2013
Solemnity of Mary, the Holy Mother of God
Galatians 4, 4-7
God's Free Children in Christ

Time! "But when the fullness of time had come, God sent his Son, born of a woman, born under the law, in order to redeem those who were under the law, so that we might receive adoption as children (v. 4)."

Proof! There is proof of our adoption.

Our loving heavenly Father has sent the Spirit of Jesus, his Son, into our heart of hearts to cry out "Abba!"

"Abba." "Father." "Papa." "Daddy." We are God's beloved children, safe and secure in our Father's love and care.

We are God's heirs. Our adoption papers have been signed and sealed. It is official!

Lord Jesus, it's true! As God's children, we are your sisters and brothers. On this first day of 2013, let us begin to live from our true identity. Let us raise our heads and look up to you, our Brother, to hold our hand, and to lead us, step by step, to the house of our Father. Alleluia!

Sunday, January 6, 2013 The Epiphany of the Lord
Ephesians 3, 2-3, 5-6
Commission to Preach God's Plan

Identity! Paul knew who he was.

He knew himself. He had experienced God's transforming grace in a powerful way.

Paul knew what he was commissioned to do. He was humble and yet confident in his vocation.

Paul, the zealous Jew, referred to himself as Christ's prisoner for the sake of the Gentiles (Ephesians 3, 1). He knew he was a minister by the gift of God's amazing grace (Ephesians 3, 7). He knew that he was the least (Ephesians 3, 8) and yet God trusted him for ministry.

Vocation! Knowing his identity, Paul could confidently live out his vocation. Paul was chosen by God to proclaim a mystery, that the Gentiles were actually co-heirs with the Jews. They were not second class citizens.

The Gentiles are not to be despised. The Gentiles are members of the same body, the Body of Christ, as the Jewish believers in Jesus.

The Gentile Christians are full partners with the Jewish Christians. The Gentiles share in all of Christ's promises through the Gospel.

Lord Jesus, thank you for our identity as God's dear children. That means we are your sisters and brothers. Thank you for our vocation to come and follow YOU! The Father sent you into the world and you are sending us into the world. Thank you for the Holy Spirit who enlightens us and teaches us how to follow you. Alleluia!

Sunday, January 13, 2013 The Baptism of the Lord
Titus 2, 11-14, 3, 4-7
Transformation of Life

"For the grace of God has appeared, bringing salvation to all, training us ... to live lives that are self-controlled, upright, and godly, while we wait for the blessed hope and the manifestation of the glory of our great God and Savior, Jesus Christ (vv. 11-13)."

Saving, Training. Awaiting.

We are saved by God's grace, but we still need training. We are still in training, learning how to live for the Lord as we await his return in glory.

Lord Jesus, thank you for mercifully rescuing us, saving us, and cleansing us in the waters of baptism. Thank you for the Holy Spirit who renews us daily and teaches us how to live for you. Alleluia!

Sunday, January 20, 2013 Second Sunday in Ordinary Time
1 Corinthians 12, 4-11
Unity and Variety

"Now there are varieties of gifts, but the same Spirit; and there are varieties of services, but the same Lord; and there are varieties of activities, but it is the same God who activates all of them in everyone (vv. 4-6)."

The same Giver, the Holy Spirit, delights in giving a variety of gifts to us. There are many ways of serving the Lord, but it is the same Lord we serve.

Lord Jesus, thank you that the Holy Spirit gives us the gifts we need in order to serve you as you have called us to serve you and to follow you all the way to the house of our Father. Alleluia!

Sunday, January 27, 2013 Third Sunday in Ordinary Time
1 Corinthians 12, 12-30
One Body, Many Parts; Application to Church

Outside? Do you think you are on the outside looking in?

No. You are on the INSIDE.

We're not just out there somewhere on our own. We're not outside.

As baptized Christians, we are inside! We are IN the Body of Christ, the Church.

We belong. We are members in the deepest sense.

"For just as the body is one and has many members, and all members of the body, though many, are one body, so it is with Christ. For in the one Spirit we were all baptized into one body – Jews or Greeks, slaves or free – and we were all made to drink of one Spirit (vv. 12-13)."

Lord Jesus, thank you that we belong to you and we belong in your Body, the Church. Thank you for the Holy Spirit who teaches us that we are neither lone rangers nor prima donnas in your Body, the Church. We rejoice in you as our Head. Alleluia!

Saturday, February 2, 2013 The Presentation of the Lord
Candlemas
Hebrews 2, 14-18
Exaltation through Abasement

"Since, therefore, the children share flesh and blood, he himself likewise shared the same things, so that through death he might destroy the one who has the power of death, that is, the devil, and free those who all their lives were held in slavery by the fear of death. For it is clear that he did not come to help angels, but the descendants of Abraham. Therefore, he had to become like his brothers and sisters in every respect, so that he might be a merciful and faithful high priest in the service of God, to make a sacrifice of atonement for the sins of the people. Because he himself was tested by what he suffered, he is able to help those who are being tested."

Tested! Jesus, the Son of God, who became human just like us, was still tested.

Tested! Jesus was tested through suffering. Because of his death on the Cross, he was able to " … free those who all their lives were held in slavery by the fear of death (v. 15)."

Tested! Jesus, having been tested, is now able, as our Brother and as our Great High Priest, to help us when we are being tested.

Lord Jesus, you became just like us and yet you never sinned. Thank you for helping us when we are being tested. Thank you for the Holy Spirit who steels us and strengthens us to pass through the testing with your smile upon us. Thank you for forgiving us when we fail and for sending us out again in your service. Alleluia!

Sunday, February 3, 2013 Fourth Sunday in Ordinary Time
1 Corinthians 12, 31 - 13, 13
The Way of Love

Never! Never does love fail.

The gifts of the Holy Spirit, wonderful though they are for building up the Body of Christ, are still partial and temporary.

Love, on the hand, is called a WAY. It is more excellent. Love never fails. It is eternal.

There is so much we do not understand. 'For we now see in a mirror, dimly, but then we will see face to face. Now I know only in part; then I will know fully, even as I have been fully known. And now faith, hope, and love abide, these three; and the greatest of these is love (vv. 12-13)."

Lord Jesus, you lived the way of love. Thank you for the Holy Spirit who teaches us how to live and how to love. Alleluia!

Sunday, February 10, 2013 Fifth Sunday in Ordinary Time
1 Corinthians 15, 1-11
The Gospel Teaching

Being! We are still being saved and made whole.

"Now I would remind you ... of the good news that I proclaimed to you, which you in turn received, in which also you stand, through which also you are being saved, if you hold firmly to the message that I proclaimed to you ... (vv. 1-2)."

Tradition! Paul simply handed on what he himself had received.

"For I handed on to you as of first importance what I in turn had received: that Christ died for our sins in accordance with the scriptures, and that he was buried, and that he was raised on the third day in accordance with the scriptures, and that he appeared to Cephas [Peter] and then to the twelve (vv. 3-5)."

Grace! Paul referred to himself as the least of the apostles because he had persecuted Christ by persecuting the Church (v. 9). Still, he was deeply aware of God's grace in his life.

"But by the grace of God I am what I am, and his grace toward me has not been in vain (v. 10a)." Paul toiled and suffered to proclaim the Gospel, yet always recognized that mighty power and grace of God was with him.

Lord Jesus, in the presence of the angels we sing your praise. You have cleansed our hearts and purified us to serve you. You continue to save us, often in spite of ourselves, and to bring us to wholeness. Let us stand fast in the amazing grace you have freely given us. Alleluia!

JANIS WALKER — SECOND READING

> Wednesday, February 13, 2013 Ash Wednesday
> 2 Corinthians 5, 20 - 6, 2
> The Ministry of Reconciliation; The Experience of the Ministry

"So we are ambassadors for Christ, since God is making his appeal through us; we entreat you on behalf of Christ, be reconciled to God. For our sake he made him to be sin who knew no sin, so that in him we might become the righteousness of God (vv. 20-21)."

Ambassadors! We are ambassadors for Christ.

We recently saw a 1935 Shirley Temple film in which Shirley starred as a little orphan. In spite of all her trials in the orphanage, she was still happy and gave happiness to others.

This Lent, we are called beyond happiness into joy. We face the fact that God the Father actually made Jesus, his beloved, sinless Son, to BECOME sin for our sakes.

Why? How could a loving Father allow that?

"For our sake he made him to be sin who knew no sin, so that in him we might become the righteousness of God (v. 21)."

Now! Now is the right time. Now is the acceptable time. Now is our "day" of salvation and wholeness.

Lord Jesus, thank you for the Holy Spirit who breathes new life into us as we begin our Lenten journey to Easter. Thank you for becoming sin for us so that we might be filled with the very holiness and righteousness of God. Thank you for hearing the cry of our heart and for helping us to follow you all the way to the Cross. Thank you for walking beside us in this joyful Lenten springtime.

> Sunday, February 17, 2013 First Sunday of Lent
> Romans 10, 8-13
> Righteousness Based on Faith

" 'The word is near you, on your lips and in your heart' (that is, the word of faith that we proclaim); because if you confess with your lips that Jesus is Lord and believe in you heart that God raised him from the dead, you will be saved. For one believes with the heart and so is justified, and one confesses with the mouth and so is saved. The Scripture says, 'No one who believes in him will be put to shame.' For there is no distinction between Jew and Greek; the same Lord is Lord of all and is generous to all who call on him. For, 'Everyone who calls on the name of the Lord shall be saved.' "

No one! No one who trustingly believes in Jesus will ever be put to shame.

Everyone! Everyone who calls on the name of the Lord Jesus Christ will be saved and will be made whole.

Lord Jesus, let us be bold and confident to believe that God truly raised you from the dead and to proclaim you as LORD! We call upon you today and thank you for the Holy Spirit who will teach us more about you and how we are to follow you through this Lenten springtime.

Sunday, February 24, 2013 Second Sunday of Lent
Philippians 3, 17 - 4, 1
Wrong Conduct and Our Goal; Live in Concord

Goal! The recent Superbowl, with all its frenzy and hype, portrayed a certain kind of life, a certain kind of goal.

Goal! As Christians, we are called to another kind of goal, a different goal.

Eyes on Jesus! Aware of our passport! We are citizens of HEAVEN and it is to heaven that we traveling.

St. Paul referred to his goal when he wrote " …this one thing I do, forgetting those things that are behind, and reaching forth unto those things which are before, I press toward the mark for the prize of the high calling of God in Jesus Christ (Philippians 3, 13-14, KJV)."

Lord Jesus, let us never be counted among the enemies of your Cross. Let us not live by being fixated on earthly matters. You will change or earthly body to be like your glorified body. Let us look to you this Lent and stand firm in our trust in you.

Sunday, March 3, 2013 Third Sunday of Lent
1 Corinthians 10, 1-6, 10-12
Warning against Overconfidence

"I do not want you to be unaware, brothers and sisters, that our ancestors were all under the cloud, and all passed through the sea, and all were baptized into Moses in the cloud and in the sea, and all ate the same spiritual food, and all drank the same spiritual drink. For they drank from the spiritual rock that followed them, and the rock was Christ.

Nevertheless, God was not pleased with most of them, and they were struck down in the wilderness. Now these things occurred as examples for us, so that we might not desire evil as they did (vv. 1-6)."

Moses! Our Hebrew ancestors in the desert were baptized into Moses. They were nourished according to the Lord's supernatural provision.

Why was the Lord so displeased with them? They desired what was evil. They complained. They committed idolatry. They indulged in immorality. They were presumptuous and tested the Lord. Some of them perished in the wilderness.

Christ! We have been baptized into Christ! Our baptism is meant to bring us into new life. We are no longer under law, but under grace (Romans 6, 14).

"Do you not know that all of us who have been baptized into Christ Jesus were baptized into his death? Therefore we have been buried with him by baptism into death, so that, just as Christ was raised from the dead by the glory of the Father, so we too might walk in newness of life (Romans 6, 3-4)."

We are called to live lives of holiness and purity. "Therefore, do not let sin exercise dominion in your mortal bodies, to make you obey their passions. No longer present your members to sin as instruments of wickedness, but present yourselves to God as those who have been brought from death to life … (Romans 6, 12-13)."

"We are cautioned against presumption. "So if you think you are standing, watch out that you do not fall. No testing has overtaken you that is not common to everyone. God is faithful, and he will not let you be tested beyond your strength, but with the testing he will also provide the way out so that you may be able to endure it (1 Corinthians 10, 12-13)."

Lord Jesus, as we continue our journey through Lent, let us cling trustingly to you. It is only in you that we stand secure.

Sunday, March 10, 2013 Fourth Sunday of Lent (Laetare Sunday)
2 Corinthians 5, 17-21
The Ministry of Reconciliation

New! "So, if anyone is in Christ, there is a new creation: everything old has passed away; see, everything has become new (v, 17)!"

"And all things are of God, who has reconciled us to himself by Jesus Christ, and hath given to us the ministry of reconciliation … God was in Christ, reconciling the world unto himself, not imputing their trespasses unto them … (vv. 18, 19a,b KJV)."

All this is from God, who reconciled us to himself through Christ, and has given us the ministry of reconciliation. We are ambassadors for Christ (vv. 17-19a, 20a).

Sin. What about our sins and our failures? How can we represent Christ when we know how sinful we are?

Jesus, the sinless One, took our sins into himself. "For our sake he made him to be sin who knew no sin, so that in him we might become the righteousness of God (v. 21)."

Lord Jesus, we cannot fully comprehend that you, the sinless Lamb of God, actually BECAME sin so that we might become righteous. You took all our sins into yourself and you died on the altar of the Cross. We are now reconciled to God because of what you did for us. We are now free to be your ambassadors and to represent you to others who need to know about your mercy. We are free to exercise the ministry of reconciliation that you have entrusted to us. Thank you for the Holy Spirit who will continue to teach us about what you have done for us and how we are called to live for you.

Sunday, March 17, 2013 Fifth Sunday of Lent
Philippians 3, 8-14
Righteousness from God; Forward in Christ

Forget! Continue the race! Remember the goal!

Paul had to learn to concentrate his energy. It was essential not to be controlled by the past. It was essential to "forget" the past in order to continue with his current ministry assignment. " … this one thing I do, forgetting those things that are behind, and reaching forth unto those things that are before, I press toward the mark for the prize of the high calling of God in Christ Jesus (vv. 13, 14 KJV)."

Paul was intent, in single-minded pursuit of his goal. He had no time to look back.

What was the goal? What was the prize he was pursuing so earnestly?

The goal was ultimately his own resurrection from the dead, which is also our goal. The goal was the prize of God's call, God's calling in Christ.

Everything else was, by comparison, mere rubbish, when compared to this prize.

"More than that, I regard everything as loss because of the surpassing value of knowing Christ Jesus my Lord. For his sake I have suffered the loss of all things, and I regard them as rubbish, in order that I may gain Christ … (vv. 8)."

What did Paul really want? "I want to know Christ and the power of his resurrection and the sharing of his sufferings by becoming like him in his death, if somehow I may attain the resurrection from the dead (vv. 10-11)."

Lord Jesus, thank you for inviting us to bring to you all our sins and failings so that we may receive your forgiveness and healing. Thank you for the powerful sacrament of reconciliation in which you listen to us and shower us with your mercy. Thank you for inviting us this Lent to reach out to you, to learn to know you more deeply, and to trust you. YOU are our goal. You are our prize. Thank you for molding us this Lent more and more into your glorious image.

Tuesday, March 19, 2013 St. Joseph
Romans 4, 13, 16-18, 22
Inheritance through Faith

Abraham! The father of all of us is Abraham.

We are among " … those who share the faith of Abraham (for he is the father of all of us, as it is written, 'I have made you the father of many nations') – in the presence of the God in whom he believed, who gives life to the dead and calls into existence the things that do not exist (vv. 16b-17)."

How did Abraham, our father in the faith, put his faith into practice? He BELIEVED!

"Hoping against hope, he believed that he would become 'the father of many nations.' according to what was said, 'So numerous shall your descendants be.' He did not weaken in faith when he considered his own body, which was already as good as dead (for he was about a hundred years old), or the when he considered the barrenness of Sarah's womb. No distrust made him waver concerning the promise of God, but he grew strong in his faith as he gave glory to God, being fully convinced that God was able to do what he had promised (vv. 18-21)."

We may think "Well, that's fine for Abraham, but what about us?" We are still called to BELIEVE!

Remember when the people asked Jesus "What must we do to perform the works of God? Jesus answered them, 'This is the work of God, that you believe in him whom he [God] has sent (John 6, 28-29).'" This kind of belief is a radical trust in the LORD!

Lord Jesus, I have hoped against hope for so long, so long, so long. Please help me this Lent to continue to hope in a strong and active way. Help me to trust you in a stronger and more active way. Thank you that you will not disappoint me. Let me honor you with my trust and obedience.

> Sunday, March 24, 2013 Palm Sunday of the Lord's Passion
> Philippians 2, 6-11
> Pleas for Unity and Humility

"Let the same mind be in you that was in Christ Jesus, who, though he was in the form of God, did not regard equality with God as something to be exploited, but emptied himself, taking the form of a slave, being born in human likeness. And being found in human form, he humbled himself and became obedient to the point of death—even death on a cross (vv. 2-8)."

Human. Human. Human.

Jesus, Son of GOD, was truly divine. Yet he set aside his true identity and the privileges of his divinity, in order to come to us and to be fully human like us.

Jesus even came as a lowly servant, a slave. His humility defies understanding.

He even humbled himself and accepted his agony in the Garden of Gethsemane, and his cruel death on the Cross for us.

Above! Because of his radical humility, God the Father has exalted his beloved Son by giving him the name above all names.

"Therefore God also highly exalted him and gave him the name that is above every name, so that at the name of Jesus every knee should bend, in heaven and on earth and under the earth, and every tongue should confess that Jesus Christ is Lord, to the glory of God the Father (vv. 9-11)."

Lord Jesus, as we enter Holy Week, let us set aside our ideas of how to follow you. Take our hand and lead us through this week. Take our heart and set us free to follow you. Let us experience your love and your presence as we gaze steadily into your eyes.

Thursday, March 28, 2013 Holy Thursday
1 Corinthians 11, 23-26
Tradition of the Institution

Paul handed on to other Christians what he himself had received from the Lord.

"For I received from the Lord what I also handed on to you, that the Lord Jesus on the night when he was betrayed took a loaf of bread, and when he had given thanks, he broke it and said, 'This is my body that is for you. Do this in remembrance of me.' In the same way he took the cup also, after supper, saying, "This cup is the new covenant in my blood. Do this, as often as you drink it, in remembrance of me.' For as often as you eat this bread and drink the cup, you proclaim the Lord's death until he comes (vv. 23-26)."

Lord Jesus, thank you for the privilege of proclaiming your death until you come to us in glory. Thank for giving us your own life.

Friday, March 29, 2013 Good Friday of the Lord's Passion
Hebrews 4, 14-16, 5, 7-9
Jesus, Compassionate High Priest

Hold on! Hold fast!

Jesus is here with us.

Jesus is our gentle, compassionate Good Shepherd.

Jesus is the pure Lamb of God who came to save us, to rescue us, to take away our sins.

Jesus is our High Priest who know us through and though and understands us.

"In the days of his flesh, Jesus offered up prayers and supplications, with loud cries and tears, to the one who was able to save him from death, and he was heard because of his reverent submission. Although he was a Son, he learned obedience through what he suffered; and having been made perfect, he became the source of eternal salvation for all who obey him, having been designated by God a high priest … (Hebrews 5, 7-10a)."

Lord Jesus, we hold onto you and cast ourselves upon your mercy. Thank you for strengthening us to follow you, obey you, and to trust you to take us Home to our loving Father.

Sunday, March 31, 2013
Easter Sunday of the Resurrection of the Lord
Colossians 3, 1-4
Mystical Death and Resurrection

Above! Above! Above!

We still live on the earth and yet we are already mystically risen with Christ.

"So if you have been raised with Christ, seek the things that are above, where Christ is, seated at the right hand of God. Set your minds on things that are above, not on things that are on earth, for you have died, and your life is hidden with Christ in God. When Christ who is your life is revealed, then you also will be revealed with him in glory (Colossians 3, 1-4)."

Lord Jesus, we rejoice in your triumph, your Easter victory. You trusted your Father all the way to the Cross and now you are with your Father in the heavenly realm. Thank you that our life is mysteriously hidden with you. We are here on earth and yet we are already with you in the heavenlies. Thank you for the Holy Spirit who strengthens us to continue to live for you here on earth, knowing that we will live forever with you in glory. ALLELUIA! ALLELUIA! ALLELUIA!

Sunday, April 7, 2013   Second Sunday of Easter
Divine Mercy Sunday
Revelation 1, 9-13, 17-19
The First Vision

Persecution. Kingdom. Endurance.

"I, John, your brother who share with you in Jesus the persecution and the kingdom and the patient endurance, was on the island called Patmos ... (v. 9)."

Exile, John was exiled on the island of Patmos because he had proclaimed the word of God.

In his exile, John saw JESUS! The risen Lord Jesus Christ appeared to him and told him not to be afraid, but to write.

"When I saw him, I fell at his feet as though dead. But he placed his right hand on me, saying, 'Do not be afraid; I am the first and the last, and the living one. I was dead, and see, I am alive forever and ever; and I have the keys .... Now write what you have seen ... (vv. 17-19a)."

Lord Jesus, thank you that you are always with us when we suffer for proclaiming you. You hold the keys to our life, our ministry, our death, and our new Life with you and the Father in heaven. We long for the time when our Father's kingdom will come and his will indeed will be done on earth as it is in heaven. Thank you for the Holy Spirit who is strengthening us today to endure and to continue to bear witness to you with confidence and courage. ALLELUIA!

Monday, April 8, 2013 The Annunciation of the Lord
Hebrews 10, 4-10
One Sacrifice instead of Many

"Sacrifice and offering you do not want; but ears open to obedience you gave me (Psalm 40, 7a)."

Jesus came to do GOD's will. "See, God, I have come to do your will, O God (v. 2a)."

"And it is by God's will that we have been sanctified through the offering of the body of Jesus Christ once for all (v. 10)."

One valid sacrifice. Jesus himself was the Lamb of God whose sacrifice took away our sins.

Mary, the Mother of Jesus, also freely agreed to accept God's plan for her. "Here I am, the servant of the Lord; let it be with me according to your word (Luke 1, 38)."

Lord Jesus, we are here to do your will and to fulfill your plan for us. Thank you for the Holy Spirit who gives us the power and the strength to live for you. Thank you for being with us each step of the way as we continue our pilgrimage to the house of our Father. ALLELUIA!

Sunday, April 14, 2013 Third Sunday of Easter
Revelation 5, 11-14
The Scroll and the Lamb

Vision! John wrote what he saw.

In John's vision, he saw angels and elders and living creatures surrounding the throne of God. In the midst of this scene, he saw a Lamb (Revelation 5, 6).

Singing! The angels and the others surrounding the throne sang to the Lamb, "Worthy is the Lamb that was slain to receive power, and riches, and wisdom, and strength, and honour, and glory, and blessing (v. 12 KJV)."

Heaven and earth! Under the earth and in the sea. John wrote of what he heard.

"Then I heard every creature in heaven and on earth and under the earth and in the sea, and all that is in them, singing, 'To the one seated on the throne and to the Lamb be blessing and honor and glory and might forever and ever!' And the four living creatures said 'Amen!' " And the elders fell down and worshiped (vv. 13,14)."

Amen, indeed.

Lord Jesus, we join the angels and all the company of heaven, the great cloud of witnesses, in singing to you and worshipping you as the Lamb of God. All honor and glory to you, our Lamb and our Shepherd. ALLELUIA!

Sunday, April 21, 2013 Fourth Sunday of Easter
Revelation 7, 9, 14-17
Triumph of the Elect

Vision! John continues to write what he saw.

A multitude in white, survivors of the time of great suffering. They were holding palm branches and standing before the Lamb.

"These are they who have come out the great ordeal; they have washed their robes and made them white in the blood of the Lamb. For this reason they are before the throne of God, and worship him day and night within his temple, and he who is seated on the throne will shelter them. They will hunger no more, and thirst no more; the sun will not strike them, nor any scorching heat; for the Lamb at the center of the throne will be their shepherd and he will guide them to springs of the water of life, and God will wipe away every tear from their eyes (vv. 14-17)."

Lord Jesus, you are our Lamb and you are our Shepherd. We praise you and we glorify you. Thank you for the Holy Spirit who is leading us through all the trials of our life on earth to the house of our Father in heaven where we will praise you forever and ever. ALLELUIA!

Sunday, April 28, 2013 Fifth Sunday of Easter
Revelation 21, 1-5
The New Heaven and the New Earth

New! New! New!

John continues to tell us of his vision. "Then I saw a new heaven and a new earth; for the first heaven and the first earth had passed away …. And I saw the holy city, the new Jerusalem, coming down out of heaven from God, prepared as a bride adorned for her husband (vv. 1-2)."

John heard a voice from the throne of God reassuring us that God will dwell with us and will make all things new (vv. 3, 5). "Death will be no more; mourning and crying and pain will be no more …. (v. 4)."

Lord Jesus, we have grown weary of the old ways which do not reflect you. The old violence. The old hatred. The old way of trying to justify ourselves. We look to you and rejoice that you, in your Easter victory, have made everything new! We pray with joy and confidence for your kingdom to come and for your will to be done on earth as it is in heaven. We glorify you. ALLELUIA!

Sunday, May 5, 2013 Sixth Sunday of Easter
Revelation 22, 12-14, 16-17, 20
The New Jerusalem

Jesus said, "See, I am coming soon; my reward is with me, to repay according to everyone's work. I am the Alpha and the Omega, the first and the last, the beginning and the end. It is I, Jesus, who sent my angel to you with this testimony for the churches. I am the root and the descendant of David, the bright morning star (vv. 12, 13, 16)."

Lord Jesus, thank you that you are coming soon! You are the One we have been waiting for and longing to see. We will see you in all your glory and majesty. Thank you for the Holy Spirit who strengthens us to live for you and to complete the assignment you have entrusted to us. Thank you that we will live forever with you in the spacious mansion of our Father. ALLELUIA!

Sunday, May 12, 2013 The Ascension of the Lord
Ephesians 1, 17-23
Unity of Church in Christ; The Church as Christ's Body

Prayer! Paul prayed unceasingly for the Church.

How did he pray? With thanksgiving first of all. "I do not cease to give thanks for you as I remember you in my prayers (v. 16)."

How did he pray next? With fervent petition.

"I pray that the God of our Lord Jesus Christ, the Father of glory, may give you a spirit of wisdom and revelation as you come to know him, so that, with the eyes of your heart enlightened, you may know what is the hope to which he has called you ... and what is the immeasurable greatness of his power for us who believe.... God put this power to work in Christ when he raised him from the dead and seated him at his right hand in the heavenly places .... And he has put all things under his feet and has made him the head over all things for the church, which is his body... (vv. 17-23)."

Lord Jesus, we live too low. We set our sights too low. We live as prisoners of low expectations. We don't see. We pray to you to lift the eyes of our hearts this day to know that you have truly ascended, mission gloriously accomplished, to the place of honor beside your Father and our Father in heaven. Thank you for the Holy Spirit who patiently teaches us to know you better and strengthens us to worship you and to continue to follow you Home. ALLELUIA!

Sunday, May 19, 2013 Pentecost Sunday
Romans 8, 8-17
The Flesh and the Spirit; Children of God through Adoption

"If the Spirit of him who raised Jesus from the dead dwells in you, he who raised Christ from the dead will give life to your mortal bodies also through the Spirit that dwells in you. For all who are led by the Spirit of God are children of God (vv. 11, 14)."

Come Holy Spirit! You raised our crucified Lord Jesus Christ from the dead. Thank you for giving life to us. Thank you for leading us and teaching us to call God our Abba, our dear Father. Thank you for strengthening us to suffer with Christ and to be glorified with Christ. ALLELUIA!

Sunday, May 26, 2013 The Most Holy Trinity
Romans 5, 1-5
Faith, Hope, and Love

Peace! It is though Jesus that we have peace with God.

Justified! We have been justified by placing our trust in Jesus.

A new land! Now we are truly living in the land of GRACE.

Now that we are living in a new land, a new state, a state of grace, we can boast. We can boast not only of the glory of God, but we can also boast in our hardships, our afflictions, and our suffering.

We are learning, through suffering, to endure. Our character, tried and tested in the furnace of suffering, is being proven.

Hope! Hope, not dead after all, springs forth. This hope does not disappoint because the Holy Spirit has poured God's love into our hearts.

Lord Jesus, thank you for the Holy Spirit who is guiding us and teaching us how to live for you and how to glorify you as we continue our pilgrimage to our Father in heaven. Alleluia!

Sunday, June 2, 2013 The Most Holy Body and Blood of Christ
1 Corinthians 11, 23-26
Tradition of the Institution

"For I received from the Lord what I also handed on to you, that the Lord Jesus on the night when he was betrayed took a loaf of bread, and when he had given thanks, he broke it and said, 'This is my body that is for you. Do this in remembrance of me.' In the same way he took the cup also, after supper, saying, 'This cup is the new covenant in my blood. Do this, as often as you drink it in remembrance of me. For as often as you eat this bread and drink the cup, you proclaim the Lord's death until he comes (1 Corinthians 11, 23-26)."

Remembrance. The Greek word used here for remembrance is "anamnesis."

Anamnesis. This is a powerful word. It is not the same as looking at an old photo and saying, "Oh, yeah, I remember that dinner."

The sacrifice of Jesus is not merely "remembered." It is truly made present.

"Through the Mass, then, the sacrifice of the cross is made present and is continued through the centuries and the event of redemption is made present. Every time we celebrate the eucharist we are entering into Jesus' experience of death and of its meaning for him and for us (<u>A New Look at the Sacraments</u> by William J Bausch, p. 132)."

Lord Jesus, thank you for taking us as you took the bread at the Last Supper and praying for us and over us. Thank you for blessing us. Thank you even for breaking us and then giving us as food for your hungry sheep and lambs. Thank you for the privilege of being, for our sated and starving world, broken bread and poured out wine. Thank you for the privilege of being heralds of your return in glory. Alleluia!

Friday, June 7, 2013 The Most Sacred Heart of Jesus
Romans 5, 5b-11
Faith, Hope, and Love

The Holy Spirit! Through the Holy Spirit, God's love has been poured into our hearts. God's love " ... is shed abroad in our hearts ... (v. 5b KJV)." The love of God is actively "gushing" into our hearts, according to the Greek verb used in this verse.

Jesus! Our Lord Jesus Christ, knowing that we were completely helpless to save ourselves, died for us. He died for us when we were still sinners, because he knew we needed him and we could not save ourselves.

The Father in heaven! Our holy and loving Father in heaven has made it possible for us to be reconciled to him because of the death of his sinless Son, Jesus, on our behalf.

We were once God's enemies because of our sins, but, now, because of the death of Jesus, we are actually reconciled to God the Father. We are saved and we are in the process of becoming whole.

Lord Jesus, thank you that the Holy Spirit continues to teach us how to live as we continue our pilgrimage to the house of our Father. Let our lives reflect the holy love that has been lavishly poured into our hearts. Alleluia!

Sunday, June 9, 2013 Tenth Sunday in Ordinary Time
Galatians 1, 11-19
Paul's Defense of His Gospel; His Call by Christ

Jesus! Paul, who had violently persecuted Christians, received an astonishing revelation of the risen Lord Jesus Christ. Paul was commissioned to proclaim Christ to the Gentiles.

This experience was a cosmic shift for Paul. He went away. For years. As he stated, " … I did not confer with any human being (v. 16c)."

Active ministry would come later. This was a time for Paul to be enclosed with Christ alone.

Lord Jesus, we tend to become excited when it is clear that you are active in our lives. You are always active in our lives, even when we think nothing is happening. Let us learn to be still and to allow you to continue to speak to us. Let us learn to listen to you and to speak only as the Holy Spirit directs us. Alleluia!

Sunday, June 16, 2013 Eleventh Sunday in Ordinary Time
Galatians 2, 16, 19-21
Faith and Works

St. Paul wrote, " I have been crucified with Christ; and it is no longer I who live, but it is Christ who lives in me. And the life I now live in the flesh I live by faith in the Son of God, who loved me and gave himself for me (vv. 19b-20)."

So it was with St. Paul. So it is with us, as baptized Christians.

"Do you not know that all of us who have been baptized into Christ Jesus were baptized into his death? Therefore we have been buried with him by baptism into death, so that, just as Christ was raised from the dead by the glory of the Father, so we too might walk in newness of life (Romans 6, 3, 4)."

Lord Jesus, thank you for the Holy Spirit who teaches us that you are really are living in us! You love us so much and you gave yourself completely to us. Let us rejoice in you as we continue our pilgrimage to the heavenly Jerusalem. Alleluia!

Sunday, June 23, 2013 Twelfth Sunday in Ordinary Time
Galatians 3, 26-29
What Faith Has Brought Us

Out of bondage and into freedom! Out of captivity to sin and into radical freedom to live in a new way.

" … in Christ Jesus you are all children of God through faith. As many of you as were baptized into Christ have clothed yourselves with Christ. There is no longer Jew or Greek, there is no longer slave or free, there is no longer male and female; for all of you are one in Christ Jesus. And if you belong to Christ, then you are Abraham's offspring, heirs according to the promise (Galatians 3, 26-29)."

Faith! It is through faith in Christ that we are God's children.

Baptism! We are baptized into Christ. We are clothed with Christ.

One! Regardless of our external differences, we are now truly one in Christ.

Abraham! Abraham? Since we belong to Christ, we are also Abraham's descendants and heirs.

Abraham "For this reason it depends on faith, in order that the promise may rest on grace and be guaranteed to all his descendants, not only to the adherents of the law but also to those who share the faith of Abraham (for he is the father of all of us, as it is written, 'I have made you the father of many nations' – in the presence of the God in whom he believed, who gives life to the dead and calls into existence the things that do not exist (Romans 4, 16-17)."

Lord Jesus, we rejoice in you and in all the benefits bestowed on us through our trust in you and through our baptism into you. Thank you that we are actually clothed with YOU! We belong to you and we are thereby Abraham's descendants. Let us live in the joy of what you have accomplished for us as we daily draw closer to our true home in the heavenly Jerusalem. Alleluia!

Monday, June 24, 2013 The Nativity of John the Baptist
Acts 13, 22-26
Paul's Address in the Synagogue

Herald! John the Baptist was the herald for the coming of Christ.

It was John's vocation to proclaim baptism. This was a baptism of repentance, to prepare the people for their Savior.

John knew he was and who he was not. He told the people that the One they were truly waiting for would follow him. He was there only to prepare the way.

Lord Jesus, sometimes we become fixated on your messenger, your herald. YOU are the one we long for and you are the one for whom we yearn. You are here! You are already here. You are with us in the Person of the Holy Spirit. Thank you for the Holy Spirit who leads us to repentance. Thank you for your eagerness to forgive us, to cleanse us, and to continue to send us out as your heralds as we rejoice that you will return in glory. Alleluia!

Saturday, June 29, 2013 Saints Peter and Paul
2 Timothy 4, 6-8, 17-18
Reward for Fidelity; Paul's Loneliness

Poured! On June 7, we read about the love of God being poured out into our hearts by the Holy Spirit (Romans 5, 5).

Poured! Today we read the words of Paul whose very life was poured out for Christ's flock.

"As for me, I am already being poured out as a libation, and the time of my departure has come. I have fought the good fight, I have finished the race, I have kept the faith. From now on there is reserved for me the crown of righteousness, which the Lord, the righteous judge, will give me on that day, and not only to me but also to all who have longed for his appearing (vv. 6-8)."

Paul had suffered greatly in his ministry. He suffered terrible misunderstanding, rejection, and cruelty from those he had come to serve.

"At my first defense, no one came to my support, but all deserted me. May it not be counted against them! But the Lord stood by me and gave me strength, so that through me the message might be fully proclaimed .... So I was rescued from the lion's mouth. The Lord will rescue me from every evil attack and save me for his heavenly kingdom. To him be the glory forever and ever. Amen (vv. 16 -18)."

Poured! Those who have offered their lives for the service of Christ and the Church prostrate themselves before the altar. We pray for them and ask all the saints to pray for them.

Lord Jesus, thank you for the Holy Spirit who pours out your love to us so that you can then freely pour us out for others. Thank you for the privilege of being your broken bread and poured out wine to feed and to refresh your flock. Alleluia!

Sunday, June 30, 2013 Thirteenth Sunday in Ordinary Time
Galatians 5, 1, 13-18
The Importance of Faith; Freedom for Service

"For freedom Christ has set us free. Stand firm, therefore, and do not submit again to a yoke of slavery (v. 1)."

Me or thee? Christ has set me free to serve you, instead of merely caving into my own wishes and serving myself.

St. Paul gets pretty graphic in this passage. "For the whole law is summed up in a single commandment, 'You shall love your neighbor as yourself.' If, however, you bite and devour one another, take care that you are not consumed by one another (vv. 13-15)."

So how do we make the transition from serving self to serving others? The Holy Spirit!

"Live by the Spirit … and do not gratify the desires of the flesh (v. 16). We are called to be led by the Holy Spirit (v. 18).

Lord Jesus, thank you for your patience with us as we are learning to live by your Holy Spirit and to be guided by your Holy Spirit. Alleluia!

Sunday, July 7, 2013 Fourteenth Sunday in Ordinary Time
Galatians 6, 14-18
Final Appeal

Paul wrote " … God forbid that I should glory, save in the cross of our Lord Jesus Christ, by whom the world is crucified unto me and I unto the world (v. 14 KJV)."

The cross. Paul truly saw himself nailed to the cross with Jesus.

"I have been crucified with Christ; and it is no longer I who live, but it is Christ who lives in me. And the life I now live in the flesh I live by faith in the Son of God, who loved me and gave himself for me (Galatians 2, 19b-20)."

Lord Jesus, we were nailed to the cross with you. Our old life is gone. We belong to you and we are free to live the new life you died to give us. We GLORY in your holy cross! Through your cross, this passing world is crucified to us. We are living a new life with you. We are new creations because of your cross. Let us live out our time in this world marked with your sacrificial love. Alleluia!

Sunday, July 14, 2013 Fifteenth Sunday in Ordinary Time
Colossians 1, 15-20
The Preeminence of Christ; His Person and His Work

Snap! Snap a photo of Jesus and you will see God.

Jesus! Jesus is the shining image of the majestic, invisible God.

"He is the image of the invisible God, the firstborn of all creation. He is before all things, and in him all things hold together. He is the head of the body, the church (vv. 15, 17-18)."

Lord Jesus, thank you that everything is held together in YOU! You are holding us together when all around us seems to be disintegrating. Your are the Head of your Body on earth, the Church. You have brought us peace through the shedding of your Blood on the Cross. Let us gaze on you today and let our lives shine with your glory. Alleluia!

Sunday, July 21, 2013 Sixteenth Sunday in Ordinary Time
Colossians 1, 24-28
Christ in Us

Rejoice! The apostle Paul could rejoice even in his suffering because he knew the meaning of his suffering. His suffering was linked to the suffering of Christ on behalf of the church.

For Paul, it was all about Christ. As a servant of the church, he knew he was there to proclaim Christ.

Glory! " ... Christ in you, the hope of glory. It is he whom we proclaim ... (vv. 27b, 28 a)."

Lord Jesus, thank you that you are in us and among us. YOU are our hope of glory. We pray that others grow in their knowledge of you. Let us proclaim you in our lives and with our words. All glory and honor to you, Lord Jesus Christ. Alleluia!

Sunday, July 28, 2013 Seventeenth Sunday in Ordinary Time
Colossians 2, 12-14
Sovereign Role of Christ

Christ! Buried with Christ. In our baptism, we were buried with Christ.

Christ! Raised with Christ. In our baptism, we were also raised with Christ.

God the Father raised our Lord Jesus Christ from the dead. We trust God also to raise us from the dead.

Christ! Our life, our new life, our real life is in Christ.

"And when you were dead in trespasses ... God made you alive together with him, when he forgave us all our trespasses, erasing the record that stood against us .... He set this aside, nailing it to the cross (vv. 13-14)."

Lord Jesus, thank you for the Holy Spirit who teaches us how to live the new life you have given us. Thank you that our loving Father in heaven has not only forgiven us but has also completely erased the record of our sins because of your triumph at the Cross. We are alive and free to follow you with confidence and with joy. Alleluia!

Sunday, August 4, 2013 Eighteenth Sunday in Ordinary Time
Colossians 3, 1-5, 9-11
Mystical Death and Resurrection; Renunciation of Vice

"So, if you have been raised with Christ, seek the things that are above, where Christ is, seated at the right hand of God. Set your minds on things that are above, not on things that are on earth, for you have died, and your life is hidden with Christ in God. When Christ who is your life is revealed, then you also will be revealed with him in glory (vv. 1-3)."

Above! Since we have been raised with Christ, we are called to think about and to seek what is "above."

We have "died" and our life, our real life, is above with Christ. Christ is our real life.

Glory! When Christ, who is our real life, returns in glory, we will be there and will appear with him in glory. We will be made manifest with Christ in glory.

We are called to renounce and to put to death our earthly temptations to immorality, idolatry, and falsehood (that means no more lying). Lying is not only the words we speak but also the intention to deceive.

We are actually to put on Christ (Romans 13, 14)! It is as if we stepped into a dressing room and removed our "old" self and we put on our new self, our real self, which is made in the beautiful image of our Creator.

Lord Jesus, this is much more exciting than children playing superheroes. They are temporarily transformed into someone else as soon as they put on their costumes. YOU are not a "costume." You are REAL. Thank you that we are to be clothed, to be vested, with YOU! Alleluia!

Tuesday, August 6, 2013 The Transfiguration of the Lord
2 Peter 1, 16-19
Apostolic Witness

Power! Our Lord Jesus Christ will come again with power in great glory.

Preview! Jesus gave Peter, John, and James a preview of his glory.

Prayer! Jesus took Peter, John, and James with him as he climbed up the mountain to pray.

"And while he was praying, the appearance of his face changed, and his clothes became dazzling white. Suddenly they saw two men, Moses and Elijah, talking to him. They appeared in glory and were speaking of his departure, which he was about to accomplish at Jerusalem (Luke 9, 29-31)."

Peter, James, and John saw Jesus, but a TRANSFIGURED Jesus, in his glory and majesty. They heard the voice of God the Father in heaven honoring his Son.

"Then ... came a voice that said, 'This is my Son, my Chosen; listen to him (Luke 9, 35)!'"

Be attentive and listen! As eyewitnesses of this astounding revelation, Peter and the other two witnesses are qualified to urge us to be attentive.

"You will do well to be attentive to this as to a lamp shining in a dark place, until the day dawns and the morning star rises in your hearts (v. 19b)."

Lord Jesus, we did not see you transfigured and yet the Holy Spirit shines within our hearts and continues to tell us who you really are. Thank you for the Holy Spirit who strengthens us to wait for the morning star. Alleluia!

Sunday, August 11, 2013 Nineteenth Sunday in Ordinary Time
Hebrews 11, 1-2, 8-12
Faith of the Ancients

"Now faith is the substance of things hoped for, the evidence of things not seen (v. 1 KJV)."

Go! God said to go and so Abraham went, not really knowing what in the world he was getting into and where in the world he was being called to go.

Tents! Living out his trust in God, Abraham lived in tents with Isaac and Jacob, heirs of the same promise. He was seeking the city with eternal foundations, whose architect and maker is GOD.

Isaac! Living out their radical trust in God, the elderly Abraham and his barren wife, Sarah, also elderly, became the parents of Isaac.

"Hoping against hope, he [Abraham] believed that he would become 'the father of many nations .... He did not weaken in faith when he considered his own body, which was already as good as dead (for he was about a hundred years old), or when he considered the barrenness of Sarah's womb. No distrust made him waver concerning the promise of God, but he grew strong in his faith as he gave glory to God, being fully convinced that God was able to do what he had promised (Romans 4, 18a, 19-21)."

Stars and sand! From the ancient Abraham, considered "dead," came as many descendants as the stars in the sky and the grains of sand on the seashore.

"Therefore sprang there even of one, and him as good as dead, so many as the stars of the sky in multitude, and as the sand which is by the sea innumerable (v. 12 KJV)."

Abraham is our father, too. He is "…the father of all of us…He is our father in the sight of God, in whom he believed, who gives life to the dead, and calls into being what does not exist (Romans 4, 16-17)."

Lord Jesus, what a heritage we have! We are Abraham's offspring and we are God's beloved children. You are our older Brother. The powerful Holy Spirit lives with in us. Nothing is impossible with you! Let us live this day in joyful, trusting abandonment to your amazing plans for us. In advance, we give you all the glory. Alleluia!

Thursday, August 15, 2013
The Assumption of the Blessed Virgin Mary
1 Corinthians 15, 20-27
Christ the Firstfruits

Annuciation! The annunciation to Mary. Life.

Assumption! The assumption of Mary into heaven. Life.

"If for this life only we have hoped in Christ, we are of all people most to be pitied. But in fact Christ has been raised from the dead, the first fruits of those who have died. For since death came through a human being, the resurrection of the dead has also come through a human being; for as all die in Adam, so all will be made alive in Christ (1 Corinthians 14-22)."

Yes! Mary said "yes."

The young Jewish teenage girl, Mary, said "yes" to God's plan for her life.

By the power of the Holy Spirit, she became the mother of our Lord Jesus Christ. Jesus was Son of God. Jesus was Son of Mary.

Jesus, by his death, has destroyed death. Death is referred to as an enemy. "The last enemy to be overcome is death (v. 26)."

Lord Jesus, thank you for the example of your Mother Mary in saying yes to God's plan for her life. Let us live today in joyful trust as we say our own "YES" to you. We are safe with you. You have overcome death and we are free to follow you all the way home to the house of our Father in heaven. Alleluia!

Sunday, August 18, 2013 Twentieth Sunday in Ordinary Time
Hebrews 12, 1-4
God our Father

We are not alone! Jesus has promised always to be with us (Matthew 28, 20).

We are not alone. We are also surrounded by " ... so great a cloud of witnesses (v. 1a)."

We still have a race to run, so "... let us run with perseverance the race that is set before us, looking to Jesus, the pioneer and perfecter of our faith, who for the sake of the joy that was set before him endured the cross, disregarding its shame, and has taken his seat at the right hand of the throne of God (v. 1b-2)."

We are keep our eyes on Jesus, who suffered and died for us. "Consider him [Jesus] who endured such hostility against himself from sinners, so that you may not grow weary or lose heart (v. 3)."

Lord Jesus, thank you for being with us always. Thank you for the heavenly cloud of witnesses who surround us. Thank you for the Holy Spirit who strengthens us to continue running the race you have assigned us to run. Before we know it, we will Home safe and sound. Alleluia!

Sunday, August 25, 2013 Twenty-first Sunday in Ordinary Time
Hebrews 12, 5-7, 11-13
God our Father

It has been said that the higher the calling, the longer the preparation. Also, the deeper and more grueling the preparation. The gentle, loving Lord is extremely strict with those being prepared for particular vocations.

The trials which will ensue are to be viewed as necessary preparation, discipline, and training. The aim is to bring forth righteousness in the innermost depths of the hearts of those being so sternly and meticulously trained.

"Therefore lift your drooping hands and strengthen your weak knees, and make straight paths for your feet, so that what is lame may not be put out of joint, but rather be healed (vv. 11-13)."

Lord Jesus, what are you doing?! It is taking so long, so long. It is so painful. Thank you that you love us so much and you know what you are doing. Thank you for the powerful Holy Spirit who strengthens us to submit to this rigorous training in order to serve you as you are calling us to serve you. We choose to honor you with our trust. We pray to glorify you now and forever. Alleluia!

Sunday, September 1, 2013
Twenty-second Sunday in Ordinary Time
Hebrews 12, 18-19, 22-24
Penalties of Disobedience

Jesus! Because of Jesus, our holy GOD, who is a consuming fire (Hebrews 12, 29) is approachable.

Moses was terrified at the initiation of the first covenant at Mount Sinai, saying "I tremble with fear (v. 21b)."

"But you have come to Mount Zion and to the city of the living God, the heavenly Jerusalem, and to innumerable angels in festal gathering, and to the assembly of the firstborn who are enrolled in heaven, and to God the judge of all, and to the spirits of the righteous made perfect, and to Jesus, the mediator of a new covenant … (vv. 22-24)."

We have been offered so great a gift. "See that you do not refuse the one who is speaking; for if they did not escape when they refused the one who warned them on earth, how much less will we escape if we reject the one who warns from heaven (v. 25)!"

"Therefore, since we are receiving a kingdom that cannot be shaken, let us give thanks, by which we offer to God an acceptable worship with reverence and awe (Hebrews 12, 28)."

Lord Jesus, you left the glory of heaven to come to earth to be born as a tiny, helpless infant. You are our mediator. You are the Lamb of God who died for us on the Cross to take our sins away. Yours is a new covenant. Let us place all our trust in you and live for you in this passing world. We rejoice that you will return in glory as our King to rule and to reign. Alleluia!

Sunday, September 8, 2013
Twenty-third Sunday in Ordinary Time
Philemon 9-10, 12-17
Plea for Onesimus

"Paul, a prisoner of Christ Jesus, and Timothy our brother, To Philemon our dear friend and coworker, to Apphia our sister, to Archippus our fellow soldier, and to the church in your house: Grace to you and peace from God our Father and the Lord Jesus Christ (Philemon 1-3)."

So begins the letter of the apostle Paul, imprisoned for proclaiming the Gospel. Paul is sending his beloved child in the faith, Onesimus, back home.

Paul writes movingly to plea that Onesimus be welcomed back as a brother in the Lord. "So if you consider me your partner, welcome him as you would welcome me (v. 17)."

Lord Jesus, open my heart to welcome each person who comes across my path as I would welcome you. When I feel unwelcome, thank you for the Holy Spirit who reminds me that you are my beloved older Brother and you always open your arms to welcome me. Thank you for holding my hand and leading me each day closer to my true Home where I am awaited, expected, and welcome. Alleluia!

Saturday, September 14, 2013 Triumph of the Cross
Philippians 2, 6-11
Plea for Unity and Humility

"Let this same mind be in you that was in Christ Jesus, who, though he was in the form of God, did not regard equality with God as something to be exploited, but emptied himself, taking the form of a slave, being born in human likeness. And being found in human form, he humbled himself and became obedient to the point of death –even death on a cross. Therefore God also highly exalted him and gave him the name that is above every name, so that at the name of Jesus every knee should bend, in heaven and on earth and under the earth, and every tongue should confess that Jesus Christ is Lord, to the glory of God the Father (vv. 5-11)."

He knows the way we think. He knows our fears. He knows why we struggle to prove ourselves.

Jesus did not have to prove who he was. He knew who he was. He was Son of God. And yet, he chose to be Son of Man, to be one of us.

Because he willingly, for our sake, accepted the cruel death on the Cross, God has highly exalted him. All will kneel before him. All will acknowledge that he is Lord.

Lord Jesus, we place all our trust in you. Thank you for the Holy Spirit who is teaching us how to think the way you think and to live and to die for your glory. Alleluia!

Sunday, September 15, 2013
Twenty-fourth Sunday in Ordinary Time
1 Timothy 1, 12-17
Gratitude for God's Mercy

"I am grateful to Christ Jesus our Lord, who has strengthened me, because he judged me faithful and appointed me to his service (v. 12)."

There is a small holy card, in blue and orange, with these words, "I give thanks to Christ Jesus our Lord, because he counted me trustworthy in making me his minister." This card is close to the crucifix I was given when I was received into the Roman Catholic Church on May 13, 1998. I don't remember who gave this little card to me, but I look at it and read it every day.

Trustworthy. In spite of his past, his history as a persecutor of Christians, the Lord chose Paul. The Lord considered Paul trustworthy in appointing him to his ministry as apostle to the Gentiles.

Mercy! Paul knew it was because of the Lord's mercy that he was called to this ministry.

"The saying is sure and worthy of full acceptance, that Christ Jesus came into the world to save sinners – of whom I am the foremost. But for that very reason I received mercy, so that in me ... Jesus Christ might display the utmost patience, making me an example to those who would come to believe in him for eternal life. To the King of the ages, immortal, invisible, the only God, be honor and glory, forever and ever. Amen (vv. 15-17)."

Lord Jesus, thank you for strengthening us to follow you. You called us and you know all about us. You know much we need your constant mercy and forgiveness. When we grow weary and discouraged, thank you for reminding us that you called us and that you consider us trustworthy. We give you all the honor and glory. Alleluia!

Sunday, September 22, 2013
Twenty-fifth Sunday in Ordinary Time
1 Timothy 2, 1-8
Prayers and Conduct

Pray! No matter how dark it is and no matter how desperate the situation, we are summoned to PRAY.

"First of all, then, I urge that supplications, prayers, intercessions, and thanksgivings be made for everyone, for kings and all who are in high positions, so that we may lead a quiet and peaceable life in all godliness and dignity. That is right and is acceptable in the sight of God our Savior, who desires everyone to be saved and to come to the knowledge of the truth. For there is one God; there is one mediator between God and humankind, Christ Jesus, himself human, who gave himself a ransom for all …. (vv. 1-6)."

The Lord is in charge. The Lord has power to change all people, including us!

"The king's heart is in the hand of the LORD, as the rivers of water; he turneth it whithersoever he will (Proverbs 21, 1 KJV)." The Lord can change the hearts of all in positions of authority.

Pray! Pray without anger and pray without argument (v. 8).

Lord Jesus, it is so hard to pray without anger when we see those in high positions who are authorizing what is evil. Thank you for the Holy Spirit who strengthens us to pray according to your will for all people. Thank you for the Holy Spirit who calls to remember to thank you and to continue to trust you. You triumphed over sin and death and you will triumph in this current situation. Alleluia!

Sunday, September 29, 2013
Twenty-sixth Sunday in Ordinary Time
1 Timothy 6, 11-16
Exhortations to Timothy

Pursue! St. Paul cautioned Timothy to shun the perils and pitfalls of the corrupt society around him.

Timothy, a trusted leader in the Christian community, was called to " … pursue righteousness, godliness, faith, love, endurance, gentleness (v. 11)."

Fight! Timothy was called actively to compete, to fight for the faith.

"Fight the good fight of faith; take hold of the eternal life, to which you were called and for which you made the good confession in the presence of many witnesses (v. 12)."

Paul gave Timothy is marching orders. "In the presence of God, who gives life to all things, and of Christ Jesus … I charge you to keep the commandment without spot or blame until the manifestation of our Lord Jesus Christ, which he will bring about at the right time – he who is the blessed and only Sovereign, the King of kings and Lord of lords. It is he alone who has immortality and dwells in unapproachable light, whom no one has ever seen or can see; to him be honor and eternal dominion. Amen (vv. 13d-1)."

Jesus! At the time of God's choosing, our Lord Jesus Christ will be made manifest to all.

God will highly exalt his Son "so that at the name of Jesus every knee should bend, in heaven and on earth and under the earth, and every tongue should confess that Jesus Christ is Lord, to the glory of God the Father (Philippians 2, 10-11)."

Lord Jesus, thank you for the Holy Spirit who patiently teaches us, in this passing world, how to live for your honor and glory. Alleluia!

Sunday, October 6, 2013
Twenty-seventh Sunday in Ordinary Time
2 Timothy 1, 6-8, 13-14
The Gifts Timothy Has Received

Reactivate! Rekindle!

Paul reminds Timothy to " ... rekindle the gift of God that is within you through the laying on of my hands ... (v. 6)."

It is GOD who has made us, as Christians, strong and powerful in bearing witness to him " ... God did not give us a spirit of cowardice, but rather a spirit of power and of love and of self-discipline (v. 7)."

We are not to cave in to fear or timidity as we serve the Lord. "For God hath not given to us the spirit of fear; but of power, and of love, and of a sound mind (v. 7 KJV)."

In the LORD, we are strong and loving. The Lord teaches us self control.

Hardship is part of the discipleship package. We will suffer as we bear witness to the Gospel. Paul suffered and so will we, in one way or another.

"Indeed, all who want to live a godly life in Christ Jesus will be persecuted. But as for you, continue in what you have learned and firmly believed, knowing from whom you learned it and how from childhood you have know the sacred writings that are able to instruct you for salvation through faith in Christ Jesus (2 Timothy 3, 12, 14-15)."

The Lord will give us the grace we need to serve as we are called to serve. As Paul said, " ... I know the one in whom I have put my trust, and I am sure that he is able to guard until that day what I have entrusted to him (vv. 12b)."

Lord Jesus, thank you for the Holy Spirit who strengthens us to bear our share of suffering as we bear witness to you. Alleluia!

Sunday, October 13, 2013
Twenty-eighth Sunday in Ordinary Time
2 Timothy 2, 8-13
Timothy's Conduct

Be strong! Paul refers to Timothy as his own child.

"You, then, my child, be strong in the grace that is in Christ Jesus …. Share in suffering like a good soldier of Christ Jesus (2 Timothy 2, 1a, 3)."

Remember! "Remember Jesus Christ, raised from the dead, a descendant of David – that is my gospel (v. 8)."

Because of Jesus, Paul is willing to endure being chained like a criminal. He knew that the word of God could not and can never be chained!

Paul saw the present life in its true context of eternity. "The saying is sure: If we have died with him, we will also live with him; if we endure, we will also reign with him; if we deny him, he will also deny us; if we are faithless, he remains faithful – for he cannot deny himself (vv. 11-13)."

Lord Jesus, thank you for the Holy Spirit who strengthens us to persevere in following you all the way Home to our Father in heaven. Alleluia!

Sunday, October 20, 2013
Twenty-ninth Sunday in Ordinary Time
2 Timothy 3, 14- 4,2
Paul's Example and Teaching; Solemn Charge

Paul's life illustrated the fact that all who choose to live wholeheartedly for Jesus Christ will suffer and be persecuted (v. 12)

Paul charges Timothy, to stay faithful to what he has learned. Paul reminds Timothy, his child in the faith, of the wisdom found in sacred Scripture.

"All Scripture is inspired by God and is useful for teaching, for reproof, for correction, and for training in righteousness, so that everyone who belongs to God may be proficient, equipped for every good work (v. 16)."

Proclaim the Gospel! Timothy is solemnly charged to proclaim God's word.

"In the presence of God and of Christ Jesus, who is to judge the living and the dead, and in view of his appearing and his kingdom, I solemnly urge you: proclaim the message, be persistent whether the time is favorable or unfavorable; convince; rebuke, and encourage, with the utmost patience in teaching (2 Timothy 4, 1-2)."

Lord Jesus, let us go forth into the world today and announce the Gospel. Alleluia!

Sunday, October 27, 2013 Thirtieth Sunday in Ordinary Time
2 Timothy 4, 6-8, 16-18
Reward for Fidelity; Paul's Loneliness

Poured! Paul wrote, "As for me, I am already being poured out as a libation ... v. 6)." We are sent forth as broken bread and poured out wine when we offer ourselves for God's service.

Poured out for the race! Paul rejoiced, "I have fought the good fight, I have finished the race, I have kept the faith (v. 7)."

The Lord is always with us in this race. Paul knew bitter rejection and suffering in his ministry. Still, he stayed in the race. "At my first defense no one came to my support, but all deserted me. May it not be counted against them! But the Lord stood by me and gave me strength ... So I was rescued from the lion's mouth (vv. 16, 17)."

Nearly home! Paul had lived and suffered long enough to know that victory was near. "The Lord will rescue me from every evil attack and save me for his heavenly kingdom. To him be the glory forever and ever. Amen (v. 18)."

Lord Jesus, thank you for being with us at every moment. You are standing with us and you will complete the work you have begun in us. Let us live today in joy and confidence. Alleluia!

Friday, November 1, 2013 All Saints
1 John 3, 1-3
Children of God

Now! We are God's children right now. We don't have to struggle to become who we already are.

Why struggle to justify ourselves before a world that does not know us? The world did not know God either, even when God became human and dwelt among us.

Now! We are God's children now.

"Beloved, we are God's children now; what we will be has not yet been revealed. What we do know is this: when he is revealed, we will be like him, for we will see him as he is. And all who have this hope in him purify themselves, just as he is pure (vv. 2-3)."

Our assignment now is to be pure as God is pure. As God's own dear children, we are called to purity.

Lord Jesus, thank you for the freedom and security we have in knowing who we are and whose we are. Thank you for the Holy Spirit who works deep within us to cleanse us and to purify our thoughts, our prayers, our words, and our actions. Alleluia!

Saturday, November 2, 2013 All Souls' Day
Romans 5, 5-11
Faith, Hope, and Love

Faith! "Therefore, since we have been justified by faith, we have peace with God through our Lord Jesus Christ (v. 1)."

Hope! This is the kind of hope that will not disappoint us " ... because the love of God has been poured into our hearts through the Holy Spirit that has been given to us (v. 5)."

Love! The love of God has been demonstrated for us. "... God proves his love for us in that while we were still sinners Christ died for us (v. 8)."

Jesus said, " ... I will not reject anyone who comes to me, because I came down from heaven not to do my own will but the will of the one who sent me. And this is the will of the one who sent me, that I should not lose anything of what he gave me, but that I should raise it [on] the last day (John 6, 37b-39)."

Lord Jesus, this is almost too much to comprehend! You have lived and died and you live again in order for us to live in the here and now as well as in all eternity. We praise you and place all our trust in you. You are watching over us and all those we love. Hallelujah!

Sunday, November 3, 2013 Thirty-first Sunday in Ordinary Time
2 Thessalonians 1, 11-2, 2
Prayer; Christ and the Lawless One

Uncertainty! In the face of uncertainty, how are we to live?

The Christians who lived in Thessalonica, the capital of the Roman province of Macedonia, were becoming preoccupied and confused about the date of the Lord's return in glory. Paul was giving them both wise counsel and encouragement.

Prayer! Paul assured the Thessalonians that he always prayed for them "… asking that our God will make you worthy of his call and will fulfill by his power every good resolve and work of faith, so that the name of our Lord Jesus may be glorified in you, and you in him, according to the grace of our God and the Lord Jesus Christ (vv. 11-12)."

Lord Jesus, as we too live in very difficult and uncertain times, we ask you to make us worthy of our call to follow you. Thank you that you will bring to fulfillment your purpose for our lives. Alleluia!

Saturday, November 9, 2013
The Dedication of the Lateran Basilica in Rome
1 Corinthians 3, 9-11, 16-17
The Role of God's Ministers

The Church in Corinth was experiencing issues of jealousy and rivalries. Paul was setting them straight about the role of the various ministers.

"What then is Apollos? What is Paul? Servants through whom you came to believe, as the Lord assigned to each. I planted, Apollos watered, but God gave the growth. So neither the one who plants nor the one who waters is anything, but only God who gives the growth. For we are God's servants, working together; you are God's field, God's building (vv. 5-7, 9)."

The foundation is CHRIST! "For no one can lay any foundation other then the one that has been laid; that foundation is Jesus Christ (v. 11)."

Paul continues his instruction. "Do you not know that you are God's temple and that God's Spirit dwells in you? If anyone destroys God's temple, God will destroy that person. For God's temple is holy, and you are that temple (vv. 16,17)."

Lord Jesus, thank you for the Holy Spirit who reminds us of our identity. We are God's garden and God's holy temple. You are our sure foundation. Let us remember daily that the Holy Spirit dwells within us. Alleluia!

Sunday, November 10, 2013
Thirty-second Sunday in Ordinary Time
2 Thessalonians 2, 16 - 3,5
Christ and the Lawless One; Request for Prayers

Strength! Speed!

Paul prayed for the Christians in Thessalonica to stay strong and steadfast. He also requested that they pray for him and his ministry partners so that God's word would speed ahead and that they would be rescued from the wicked.

Paul assured them, "... the Lord is faithful; he will strengthen you and guard you from the evil one. And we have confidence in the Lord concerning you, that you are doing and will go on doing the things that we command. May the Lord direct your hearts to the love of God and to the steadfastness of Christ (vv. 4-5)."

Lord Jesus, thank you for the Holy Spirit who strengthens us to continue to bear witness to you. Let your word speed forth from our lives and to bring glory to you. Alleluia!

Sunday, November 17, 2013
Thirty-third Sunday in Ordinary Time
2 Thessalonians 3, 7-12
Neglect of Work

Work! Toil. Drudgery. Day and night.

The apostles worked hard in order to support themselves. They did want to be a burden to those who benefited from their ministry.

Model! They worked in this sacrificial way in order to be an example, a role model, to the Christian community.

The apostles showed tough love, however. They knew how to confront.

"For even when we were with you, we gave you this command: Anyone unwilling to work should not eat. For we hear that some of you are living in idleness, mere busybodies, not doing any work. Now such persons we command and exhort in the Lord Jesus Christ to do their work quietly and to earn their own living. Brothers and sisters, do not be weary in doing what is right (vv. 10-13)."

Lord Jesus, forgive us when we whine about the monotony and drudgery of our work. Thank you that we have work to do in your kingdom. Thank you for the Holy Spirit who strengthens us to work and to continue to be faithful in your service and to be patient with your plan for us. Alleluia!

> Sunday, November 24, 2013 Christ the King
> Colossians 1, 12-20
> Prayer for Continued Progress
> The Preeminence of Christ: His Person and Work

Jesus! Jesus Christ our Lord! Who is he?

"He is the image of the invisible God, the firstborn of all creation; for in him all things in heaven and on earth were created, things visible and invisible, whether thrones or dominions or rulers or powers – all things have been created through him and for him. He himself is before all things, and in him all things hold together. He is the head of the body, the church; he is the beginning, the firstborn from the dead, so that he might come to have first place in everything. For in him all the fullness of God was pleased to dwell, and through him God was pleased to reconcile to himself all things, whether on earth or in heaven, by making peace through the blood of his cross (vv. 15-20)."

The Father! Our Father in heaven " … has enabled you to share in the inheritance of the saints in the light. He has rescued us from the power of darkness and transferred us into the kingdom of his beloved Son, in whom we have redemption, the forgiveness of sins (vv. 12-14)."

Lord Jesus, you are truly our King who will return in glory. You came from heaven by the power of the Holy Spirit to be with us, to be one of us, and to bring us back with you to heaven. Thank you for the Holy Spirit who reminds us that we have been delivered from the kingdom of darkness and transferred to the kingdom of light. Thank you for the Holy Spirit who strengthens us to trust you and to continue to live for your glory. Alleluia!

Thursday, November 28, 2013 Thanksgiving Day
1 Corinthians 1, 3-9
Greeting: Thanksgiving

First things first! Paul was about to confront the Christians in Corinth about various matters of concern in their community. First of all, however, he offered encouraging words of peace and grace.

Thanks! Paul thanked God for the grace given to the Corinthian Christians.

Paul reminded them that they were not lacking in spiritual gifts. He also reassured them that God would continue to strengthen them.

"He will also strengthen you to the end, so that you may be blameless on the day of our Lord Jesus Christ. God is faithful; by him you were called into the fellowship of his Son, Jesus Christ our Lord (vv. 8-9)."

Lord Jesus, thank you for the Holy Spirit who reminds us to speak words of peace and to offer thanks for those we serve. Alleluia!

Sunday, December 1, 2013 First Sunday of Advent Year A
Romans 13, 11-14
Awareness of the End of Time

Wake up!

Remember "Sleepers Wake," the hymn which begins "Wake, awake for night is flying…!" This song summons to be like the watchers on the walls.

"For our salvation is nearer now than when we first believed; the night is advanced, the day is at hand. Let us then throw off the works of darkness [and] put on the armor of light; let us conduct ourselves properly as in the day …(vv. 11-13a)."

Get dressed!

We are called to " …put on our Lord Jesus Christ, and make no provision for the desires of the flesh (v. 14)."

Lord Jesus, thank you for this call to live consciously and conscientiously before you. You are coming sooner than we think. Alleluia!

Sunday, December 8, 2013 Second Sunday of Advent
Romans 15, 4-9
Patience and Self-Denial; God's Fidelity and Mercy

Welcome! I remember a time in my life feeling very unwelcome in a particular setting. Visiting a garden shop, I was very moved by a display of many, bright, colorful, happy "Welcome" signs.

Marty Haugen's hymn, written in 1994, "All Are Welcome" immediately came to mind. I found it in <u>Breaking Bread</u> and was again very moved.

"May the God of steadfastness and encouragement grant you to live in harmony with one another, in accordance with Christ Jesus, so that together with one voice glorify the God and Father of our Lord Jesus Christ. Welcome one another, therefore, just as Christ has welcomed you, for the glory of God (vv. 5-7)."

Lord Jesus, please open our hearts to welcome others as you have welcomed us. Let us, Jew and Gentile alike, praise and glorify you. Alleluia!

Monday, December 9, 2013 The Immaculate Conception
Ephesians 1, 3-6, 11-12
The Father's Plan of Salvation; Inheritance through the Spirit

Chosen! "Blessed be the God and Father of our Lord Jesus Christ, who has blessed us in Christ with every spiritual blessing in the heavenly places, just as he chose us in Christ before the foundation of the world to be holy and blameless before him in love (vv. 3-4)."

Destined! "He destined us for adoption as his children through Jesus Christ, according to the good pleasure of his will… (v. 5)."

Inheritors! "In Christ we have also obtained an inheritance, having been destined according to the purpose of him who accomplishes all things according to his counsel and will… (v. 11)."

Lord Jesus, thank you that we are your sisters and brothers because your Abba, your Father in heaven, has adopted us. Thank you for the Holy Spirit who is teaching us how to live holy lives as we await your return in glory. Alleluia!

Sunday, December 15, 2013 Third Sunday of Ordinary Time
James 5, 7-10
Patience and Oaths

"Be patient, therefore, beloved, until the coming of the Lord. The farmer waits for the precious crop from the earth, being patient with it until it receives the early and the late rains. You also must be patient. Strengthen your hearts, for the coming of the Lord is near. Beloved, do not grumble against one another, so that you may not be judged. See, the Judge is standing at the doors! As an example of suffering and patience, beloved, take the prophets who spoke in the name of the Lord."

Lord Jesus, thank you for the Holy Spirit who is teaching us to be patient as we await your coming in glory. Let us live as good farmers who sow the seed, wait for the rain, and expect the harvest. Let us refrain from fussing and complaining about each other. We leave all matters of judgment to you. Let us persevere with courage as did the brave prophets of old. Alleluia!

Sunday, December 22, 2013 Fourth Sunday of Advent
Romans 1, 1-7
Greeting

Paul! The apostle Paul referred to himself as a slave, as Christ's slave. A slave sent out as an apostle, a slave set apart by God for the Gospel.

JESUS! The Gospel is about God's Son, Jesus. Jesus, truly human and truly the Son of God. Jesus, our Lord, who died and rose from the dead.

You and I! We are called to be holy. We are called to preach Christ, to proclaim Christ.

In the concluding rites of the Mass, the deacon or priest says, "Go and announce the Gospel of the Lord" or "Go in peace, glorifying the Lord by your life."

As Paul reminded the Christians in Corinth, "We not proclaim ourselves; we proclaim Jesus Christ as Lord and ourselves as your slaves for Jesus' sake. For it is the God who said, 'Let light shine out of the darkness,' who has shone in our hearts to give the light of the knowledge of the glory of God in the face of Jesus Christ (2 Corinthians 4, 5-6)."

Lord Jesus, you have called us to follow you. As the Father sent you into the world, so you have sent us out into the world. Thank you for the Holy Spirit who is teaching us how to live lives of holiness and how to glorify you. Alleluia!

Wednesday, December 25, 2013 The Nativity of the Lord
Hebrews 1, 1-6
The Son, Higher than the Angels; Messianic Enthronement

"Long ago God spoke to our ancestors in many and various ways by the prophets, but in these last days he has spoken to us by a Son, whom he appointed heir of all things, through whom he also created the worlds. He is the reflection of God's glory and the exact imprint of God's very being, and he sustains all things by his powerful word (vv. 1-3a)."

Do not let anyone tell you that Jesus is an angel. Jesus is not an angel.

The holy angels WORSHIP Jesus! Jesus is superior to the angels. Jesus is King.

Recall the glorious hymn, "Angels from the Realms of Glory!"

Glory! The radiant glory of God the Father shines forth from Jesus. Jesus is the imprint of the very being of God.

Jesus alone achieved the atonement for our sins. Jesus, by taking our sins within himself and dying, has cleansed us from the weight and burden of our sins.

Free! Cleansed and purified, we are free to live and to follow Jesus, our Savior.

Lord Jesus, how can we ever thank you and praise you for coming to us as God's own beloved Son? You are our Savior. We cannot live without you and your merciful love. Shine upon us and through us today. We adore you and give you all the glory, Alleluia!

Sunday, December 29, 2013 The Holy Family
Colossians 3, 12-21
Renunciation of Vice; The Christian Family

Identity! Dress code! Code of conduct!

St. Paul teaches us about identity, dress code, and code of conduct. "...As God's chosen ones, holy and beloved, clothe yourselves with compassion, kindness, humility, meekness, and patience. Bear with one another and, if anyone has a complaint against another, forgive each other; just as the Lord has forgiven you, so you also must forgive. Above all, clothe yourselves with love, which binds everything together in perfect harmony (vv. 14, 14)."

Heart code! Now that we are dressed. we are to let Christ's peace control our hearts. "And let the peace of Christ rule in your hearts, to which indeed you were called in the one body. (v. 15a)."

Thanksgiving! We are to remember always to be thankful. "And whatever you do, in word or deed, do everything in the name of the Lord Jesus, giving thanks to God the Father through him (v. 17)."

Family life! "Wives, be subject to your husbands, as is fitting in the Lord. Husbands, love your wives and never treat them harshly. Children, obey your parents in everything, for this is your acceptable duty in the Lord. Fathers, do not provoke your children, or they may lose heart (vv. 18-21)."

Lord Jesus, thank you for bringing us into your family, the Church. You are the head of the Church and you are our older Brother. Thank you for the Holy Spirit who teaches us how to follow you as you lead us each day closer to the house of our loving Father in heaven. Alleluia!

Wednesday, January 1, 2014 Mary, the Holy Mother of God
Galatians 4, 4-7
God's Free Children in Christ

Time! "But when the fullness of time had come, God sent his Son, born of a woman, born under the law, in order to redeem those who were under the law, so that we might receive adoption as children. And because you are children, God sent the Spirit of his Son into our hearts, crying 'Abba! Father! So you are no longer a slave but a child, and if a child then also an heir, through God (vv. 4-7)."

Free! We are God's beloved children. We are free to enjoy our identity. We are secure in God's love and care.

Free! We are not only God's children, but we are also God's heirs.

Free! We are free to live for God. We are free from trying to live for the approval of others.

Lord Jesus, thank you for being born of the Virgin Mary. Thank you for being born to ransom us, to buy us back out of our dismal slavery to self. Thank you for the Holy Spirit who is breathing new life into us to live as daughters and sons of our Father in heaven. We are your sisters and brothers and you are gently leading us each day closer and closer to our true Home. Alleluia!

Sunday, January 5, 2014 The Epiphany of the Lord
Ephesians 3, 2-3a, 5-6
Commission to Preach God's Plan

"This is the reason that I Paul am a prisoner for Jesus Christ for the sake of you Gentiles – for surely you have already heard of the commission of God's grace that was given me for you, and how the mystery was made known to me by revelation .... In former generations this mystery was not made known to humankind, as it has now been revealed to his holy apostles and prophets by the Spirit: that is, the Gentiles have become fellow heirs, members of the same body, and sharers in the promise in Christ Jesus through the gospel (vv. 1-3, 5-6)."

Mystery! God's amazing plan!

The Jews were especially chosen by God, yes, but the mystery of Christ is that the Gentiles are co-heirs, full-fledged members of Christ's Body, the Church, and share fully in the promises of Christ.

Lord Jesus, thank you for the Holy Spirit who reminds us of our identity and our vocation. We are sons and daughters of GOD! We are secure as God's beloved children. We are free to be instruments of God's grace to benefit others. Thank you for shining upon us and through us. Alleluia!

Sunday, January 12, 2014 The Baptism of the Lord
Acts 10, 34-38
Peter's Speech

"Then Peter began to speak to them: 'I truly understand that God shows no partiality, but in every nation anyone who fears him and does what is right is acceptable to him. You know the message he sent to the people of Israel, preaching peace by Jesus Christ – he is Lord of all. That message spread throughout Judea, beginning in Galilee after the baptism that John announced: how God anointed Jesus of Nazareth with the Holy Spirit and with power; how he went about doing good and healing all who were oppressed by the devil, for God was with him (Acts 10, 34-38)."

What is God proclaiming through your life? What is God proclaiming through my life?

Through the life of Jesus, God proclaimed PEACE!

With the Holy Spirit and with power, God anointed Jesus to do good and to heal.

Lord Jesus, thank you for our baptism in which we are sealed by the Holy Spirit. We are now marked forever as your own. Thank you for the Holy Spirit who strengthens us to follow you and to serve you. Let our lives proclaim your power and your peace. Alleluia!

Sunday, January 19, 2014 Second Sunday in Ordinary Time
1 Corinthians 1, 1-3
Greeting

Called! We are called to be holy.

All who call upon Jesus are called to holiness. We are called to live lives of purity and power.

We are standing on holy ground. The Lord is present with us and within us.

Lord Jesus, when we feel fragmented and forgotten, thank you for the Holy Spirit who gently reminds us of our vocation to holiness. You are working within us and through us, bringing us to wholeness, as we steadfastly continue our pilgrimage Home to the house of our Father in heaven. Alleluia!

Sunday, January 26, 2014 Third Sunday in Ordinary Time
1 Corinthians 1, 10-13
Groups and Slogans

Paul knew what he was called to do. He also knew what he was not called to do. He was called to proclaim the Gospel!

Erudite though he was, he was not called to preach with merely human eloquence. The attention was to be not on Paul, but on the cross of Christ.

Paul urged the Christians in Corinth to live in unity, without division. They were to have the same mind and the same purpose.

The mind of Christ! "Those who are spiritual discern all things, and they are themselves subject to no one else's scrutiny. 'For who has known the mind of the Lord so as to instruct him?' But we have the mind of Christ (1 Corinthians 2, 15-16)."

Unity! Jesus prayed for unity among his followers.

He prayed for us as well as for his first followers. "I ask not only on behalf of these, but also on behalf of those who will believe in me through their word, that they may all be one. As you, Father, are in me and I am in you, may they also be in us, so that the world may believe that you have sent me (John 17, 20-21)."

Lord Jesus, although we have just concluded the Week of Prayer for Christian Unity, we continue to pray for this unity which is clearly your will. Let our actions manifest our conviction that you are calling us to be one. Alleluia!

> Sunday, February 2, 2014 The Presentation of the Lord
> Hebrews 2, 14-18
> Exaltation through Abasement

Flesh and blood! We live in a body of flesh and blood. Jesus did, too. He came to us, not only to be with us, but also to be one of us.

We are his sisters and brothers. He became just like us " … in every respect, so that he might be a merciful and faithful high priest in the service of God, to make a sacrifice of atonement for the sins of the people (v. 17 bc)."

He was fully human. He was fully divine.

He suffered. "Because he himself was tested by what he suffered, he is able to help those who are being tested (v. 18)."

As human beings, we've always been frightened about death. So Jesus came to destroy the devil's power of death. Jesus went THROUGH death and rose triumphantly.

We are free! We are free to live and follow Jesus all through our earthly life and into eternity.

Jesus willingly humbled himself. "And being found in human form, he humbled himself and became obedient to the point of death – even death on a cross. Therefore God also highly exalted him and gave him the name that is above every name …. (Philippians 2, 8, 9)."

Now it's our turn willingly to humble ourselves. 'Humble yourselves therefore under the mighty hand of God, so that he may exalt you in due time (1 Peter 5,6)."

Lord Jesus, you are victorious! You lived and died and rose from the dead. You are living now in your glorified body in heaven with your Father. Thank you for the Holy Spirit who is strengthening us to live fearlessly and triumphantly for your glory. Alleluia!

Sunday, February 9, 2014 Fifth Sunday in Ordinary Time
1 Corinthians 2, 1-5
The Corinthians and Paul

"When I came to you, brothers and sisters, I did not come proclaiming the mystery of God to you in lofty words or wisdom. For I decided to know nothing among you except Jesus Christ, and him crucified. And I came to you in weakness and in fear and in much trembling (vv. 1-3)."

Weakness. Fear. Trembling. Can this really describe the great St. PAUL?

Instead of the zealous former persecutor of Christ and his Church, Paul had been transformed by the power of the Holy Spirit.

Paul was still zealous, but now he was zealous for the glory of God. He became obedient to serve God on God's terms. "My speech and my proclamation were not with plausible words of wisdom, but with a demonstration of the Spirit and of power, so that your faith might not rest on human wisdom but on the power of God (vv. 4-5)."

He directed all attention to Jesus Christ, the Crucified. "... I decided to know nothing among you except Jesus Christ, and him crucified (v. 2)."

Lord Jesus, thank you for the example of the transformed life of the apostle Paul. By the power of the Holy Spirit he was transformed to become a powerful preacher of your Gospel. Thank you for the Holy Spirit who is transforming us and strengthening us to live for you and to serve you on your terms. Alleluia!

Sunday, February 16, 2014 Sixth Sunday in Ordinary Time
1 Corinthians 2, 6-10
The True Wisdom

Of course, as I read this passage I remembered the beautiful song "Eye Has Not Seen," by Marty Haugen. Such peace and joy and comfort in these words.

Paul refers to the wisdom of God as "…secret and hidden, which God decreed before the ages for our glory (v. 7)." This is clearly a wisdom beyond mere human wisdom.

Paul continues, " 'What no eye has seen, nor ear heard, nor the human heart conceived, what God has prepared for those who love him'

– these things God has revealed to us through the Spirit; for the Spirit searches everything, even the depths of God. For what human being knows what is truly human except the human spirit that is within? So also no one comprehends what is truly God's except the Spirit of God (vv. 7-11)."

This is so far above our limited understanding! We need help and help is on the way in the Person of the Holy Spirit.

"Now we have received not the Spirit of the world, but the Spirit that is from God, so that we may understand the gifts bestowed on us by God (1 Corinthians 2, 12)."

Lord Jesus, thank you for the Holy Spirit who carefully examines us, knows us through and through, and guides us to live wisely in this world as we await the joy that God our Father has prepared for us. Alleluia!

Sunday, February 23, 2014   Seventh Sunday in Ordinary Time
1 Corinthians 3, 16-23
The Role of God's Ministers

"Do you not know that you are God's temple and that God's Spirit dwells in you (v. 16)?"

Paul reminds us of our identity as Christians and of our call to holiness. "If anyone destroys God's temple, God will destroy that person. For God's temple is holy, and you are that temple (v. 17)."

Paul then refers to human leaders in the church. "So let no one boast about human leaders (v. 21)." The reference is always to be to the LORD!

To the LORD! In the Old Testament, the Hebrew scriptures, there are numerous references to the duty of the priests to minister to the Lord, to serve the Lord.

"… David commanded that no one but the Levites were to carry the ark of God, for the LORD had made them to carry the ark of the LORD and to minister to him forever (1 Chronicles 15, 2)."

Paul is very clear about the role of ministry in the Church. He had previously referred to the quarreling and jealousy being evidenced by the Christians in Corinth (1 Corinthians 3, 3-5)

"I planted, Apollos watered, but God gave the growth. So neither the one who plants nor the one who waters is anything, but only God who gives the growth. For we are God's servants, working together; you are God's field, God's building (vv. 6, 7, 9)."

We are not to get caught up in all the various personalities of God's ministers. "So let one boast about human leaders. For all things are yours, whether Paul or Apollos or Cephas or the world or life or death or the present or the future – all belong to you, and you belong to Christ, and Christ belongs to God (vv. 21-23)."

There is no room to boast about human leaders "Let the one who boasts, boast in the Lord (1 Corinthians 1, 31b)."

All glory is given to the LORD! The Lord is in charge.

"For who has known the mind of the Lord so as to instruct him?" But we have the mind of Christ (1 Corinthians 2, 16)."

Lord Jesus, thank you for giving us your mind and your way of thinking. Thank you for the Holy Spirit who purifies our thoughts and leads us to act in accord with your plan. We are secure in our identity. We are God's temple. We have no need to defend ourselves or to boast. Alleluia!

Sunday, March 2, 2014 Eighth Sunday in Ordinary Time
Corinthians 4, 1-5
The Role of God's Ministers

Servants. Stewards.

Paul instructed the Christians in Corinth to regard him and the other apostles as servants and stewards. "Think of us in this way, as servants of Christ and stewards of God's mysteries (v. 1)."

Paul knew he was required to be trustworthy. However, he was not overly concerned with the opinions of others. He was not even too concerned about his opinion of himself!

"I am not aware of anything against myself, but I am not thereby acquitted. It is the Lord who judges me. Therefore do not pronounce judgment before the time, before the Lord comes, who will bring to light the things now hidden in darkness and will disclose the purposes of the heart. Then each one will receive commendation from God (vv. 4,5)."

Lord Jesus, thank you for freeing us from unhealthy concern about the approval of others and from unhealthy introspection. Thank you for the Holy Spirit who purifies our motives and strengthens us to serve you with courage and integrity. Let us have brave hearts in your service. Alleluia!

Wednesday, March 5, 2014 Ash Wednesday
2 Corinthians 5, 20 - 6,2
The Ministry of Reconciliation; The Experience of the Ministry

A story is told of a devout Christian traveling on an airplane. The person seated next to the Christian asked, "What do you do? For whom do you work?"

The answer, given with all seriousness, was, "I work for the King." The inquirer was fascinated and pursued the matter by asking, "The KING?! Really? What king?" The answer was "JESUS CHRIST THE KING."

Jesus told his disciples, "No one has greater love than this, to lay down one's life for one's friends. You are my friends if you do what I command you. I do not call you servants any longer, because the servant does not know what the master is doing; but I have called you friends, because I have made known to you everything that I have heard from my Father. You did not choose me, but I chose you (John 15, 13-16a)."

Jesus, our King, trusts us to be his friends. Jesus chooses to send us out into the world as his ambassadors.

"So we are ambassadors for Christ, since God is making his appeal through us; we entreat you on behalf of Christ, be reconciled to God (2 Corinthians 5, 20)."

Ash Wednesday! We are reminded today and every day of what our King has done for us.

We are reminded, as in the words of the song, "The King Shall Come When Morning Dawns," that Jesus, our King, will indeed return in glory.

"For our sake he made him to be sin who knew no sin, so that in him we might become the righteousness of God (2 Corinthians 5, 21)."

Called! As friends and ambassadors of our King, we are called to the ministry of reconciliation.

God " ... reconciled us to himself through Christ, and has given us the ministry of reconciliation; that is, in Christ God was reconciling the world to himself, not counting their trespasses against them, and entrusting the message of reconciliation to us (2 Corinthians 5, 19)."

Lord Jesus, you, the sinless one actually became sin. You took all our sins into yourself and you died on the Cross. On the Cross, our sins died with you. Staggering though it is, we actually share in your holiness and righteousness. You made this possible! Thank you for the Holy Spirit who is helping us to begin to comprehend this exchange. Today, let us believe that your righteousness is truly our righteousness. Let us live in this joy during this beautiful Lenten springtime. Praise to you, Lord Jesus Christ.

> Sunday, March 9, 2014 First Sunday of Lent
> Romans 5, 12-19
> Humanity's Sin through Adam; Grace and Life through Christ

"Therefore, just as sin came into the world through one man, and death came through sin, and so death spread to all because all have sinned… (v. 12).

Who is in charge? Who reigns? Who is king? Death reigned and " … exercised dominion from Adam to Moses ….(v. 14a)."

Jesus! Jesus came into the picture and changed everything.

"But the free gift is not like the trespass. For if the many died through the one man's trespass, much more surely have the grace of God and the free gift in the grace of the one man, Jesus Christ, abounded for the many (v. 15)."

Disobedience. Obedience.

Through the disobedience of one man, Adam, all were under the reign of death.

Because of the obedience of one man, Jesus, all may become righteous.

"For just as by the one man's disobedience the many were made sinners, so by the one man's obedience the many will be made righteous (v. 19)."

Lord Jesus, we are not helpless victims. Your obedience overcame the disobedience of Adam. You made it gloriously possible for us to live victoriously in this life and to live forever with you in heaven. Praise to you, Lord Jesus Christ.

Sunday, March 16, 2014 Second Sunday of Lent
2 Timothy 1, 8-10
The Gifts Timothy Has Received

Paul wrote to Timothy, "Do not be ashamed, then, of the testimony about our Lord or of me his prisoner, but join with me in suffering for the gospel, relying on the power of God, who saved us and called us with a holy calling, not according to our works but according to his own purpose and grace. This grace was given to us in Christ Jesus before the ages began, but now it has been revealed through the appearing of our Savior Christ Jesus, who abolished death and brought life and immortality to light through the gospel (2 Timothy 1, 8-10)."

We are called to bear our share of the hardships that accompany the Gospel. It is simply part of the package! The Holy Spirit gives us the strength to do this (v. 7).

Do you remember the Irish poet, Cecil Frances Alexander, who wrote "All Things Bright and Beautiful?" She wrote another poem, "Jesus Calls Us." Both of these have been set to music

As we obey the Lord, follow the Lord, and serve the Lord. we will experience suffering. All who are determined to live for Christ will suffer persecution in some way (2 Timothy 3, 12). This is part of the discipleship package.

Lord Jesus, thank you for the Holy Spirit who strengthens us to live lives of holiness. Thank you for shining upon us and through us as we go into the world to live for you and to proclaim the Gospel. Praise to you, Lord Jesus Christ.

Wednesday, March 19, 2014 St. Joseph
Romans 4, 13, 16-18, 22
Inheritance through Faith

Rich! We are crazy rich in faith and we owe a lot to our father. Our father ABRAHAM!

Abraham is " ... the father of all of us.... He is our father in the sight of God, in whom he believed, who gives life to the dead and calls into being what does not exist. He believed, hoping against hope, that he would become 'the father of many nations.... (vv. 16-18)."

Radical faith. Radical trust.

Abraham's radical faith and trust in God can be ours. "He did no doubt God's promise in unbelief; rather he was empowered by faith and gave glory to God and was fully convinced that what he had promised he was also able to do. That is why 'it was credited to him as righteousness.' But it was not for him alone that it was written that 'it was credited to him'; it was also for us, to whom it will be credited, who believe in the one who raised Jesus our Lord from the dead… (vv. 20-24)."

Lord Jesus, thank you that we may share in the faith of Abraham. Nothing is impossible with you!

Sunday, March 23, 2014 Third Sunday of Lent
Romans 5, 1-2, 5-8
Faith, Hope, and Love

Faith!

"Therefore, since we are justified by faith, we have peace with God through our Lord Jesus Christ, through whom we have obtained access to this grace in which we stand; and we boast in our hope of sharing the glory of God (vv. 1-2)."

Hope! Love!

"Hope does not disappoint us, because God's love has been poured into our hearts through the Holy Spirit that has been given to us (v. 5)."

Jesus came to our aid when we were unable to help ourselves. "For while we were still weak, at the right time Christ died for the ungodly. Indeed, rarely will anyone die for a righteous person – though perhaps for a good person someone might actually dare to die. But God proves his love for us in that while we were still sinners Christ died for us (vv. 6-8)."

Lord Jesus, thank you for coming to help us when we could not help ourselves. Thank you for the Holy Spirit who teaches us about God's love which is being continually poured into our hearts. Let us live today with faith, hope, and love. Praise to you, Lord Jesus Christ.

Sunday, March 30, 2014 Fourth Sunday of Lent
Ephesians 5, 8-14
Duty to Live in the Light

"Christ, Be Our Light!" The stirring words of Bernadette Farrell's beautiful hymn invite us to realize that indeed Christ IS our light.

"For once you were darkness, but now in the Lord you are light. Live as children of light – for the fruit of the light is found in all that is good and right and true. Try to find out what is pleasing to the Lord. Take no part in the unfruitful works of darkness, but instead expose them (vv. 8-11)."

Light and darkness! "…everything exposed by the light becomes visible, for everything that becomes visible is light (v. 13)."

We are summoned to awaken. "Sleeper, awake! Rise from the dead, and Christ will shine on you (v. 14)."

Lord Jesus, thank you for the Holy Spirit who is instructing us how to live our identity as children of the light. Thank you that your light within us is purifying us and shining through us. Praise to you, Lord Jesus Christ.

Sunday, April 6, 2014 5th Sunday of Lent
Romans 8, 8-11
The Flesh and the Spirit

The Holy Spirit.

"If the Spirit of him who raised Jesus from the dead dwells in you, he who raised Christ from the dead will give life to your mortal bodies also through his Spirit that dwells in you (v. 11)."

I recently heard a beautiful performance on You Tube of "Come, Holy Ghost," composed by the nineteenth century Belgian Jesuit priest, Fr. Louis Lambillotte. Truly these words inspire us to pray to be filled with the powerful Holy Spirit.

Lord Jesus, you know how much we need the Holy Spirit. Thank you for the Holy Spirit who is daily teaching us and strengthening us to live for you. Praise to you, Lord Jesus Christ.

Sunday, April 13, 2014 Palm Sunday of the Lord's Passion
Philippians 2, 6-11
Plea for Unity and Humility

Unity! Paul pled for unity amongst Christians, urging them to " … be of the same mind, having the same love, being in full accord and of one mind (vv. 2b)."

We are praying for unity each time we sing "One Bread, One Body," written by Fr. John Foley, S.J. Jesus prayed that we, as Christians, would be one. In his high priestly prayer, Jesus prayed, "Holy Father, protect them in your name that you have given me, so that they may be one, as we are one (John 17, 11)."

Paul then gave them the tools to live this way. "Do nothing from selfish ambition or conceit, but in humility regard others as better than yourselves. Let each of you look not to your own interests, but to the interests of others (vv. 3-4)."

The mind of Christ! "Let the same mind be in you that was in Christ Jesus, who, though he was in the form of God, did not regard equality with God as something to be exploited, but emptied himself, taking the form of a slave, being born in human likeness, And being found in human form, he humbled himself and became obedient to the point of death – even death on a cross (vv. 5-8)."

Death did not have the last word. GOD had the last word.

"Therefore God also highly exalted him and gave him the name that is above every name, so that at the name of Jesus every knee should bend, in heaven and on earth and under the earth, and every tongue should confess that Jesus Christ is Lord, to the glory of God the Father (vv. 9-11)."

Lord Jesus, forgive us when we grasp for status, recognition, and approval from others. Thank you for the Holy Spirit who reminds us to have your attitude of trust and humility. Thank you for the Holy Spirit who strengthens us to become completely obedient to our Father. Your willingness to be like us and to become obedient even to death on a Cross led to your exaltation. Thank you for the time when all will kneel before you and acknowledge that you are Lord to the glory of our Father in heaven. Praise to you, Lord Jesus Christ.

Thursday, April 17, 2014 Holy Thursday; The Lord's Supper
1 Corinthians 11, 23-26
Tradition of the Institution

"The Supper of the Lord." The text and music of this beautiful song (1994, 2012) are by Laurence Rosania. We sing it often at Mass.

This song, so meaningful to me, came to mind as I read this passage from 1 Corinthians.

"For I received from the Lord what I also handed on to you, that the Lord Jesus on the night when he was betrayed took a loaf of bread, and when he had given thanks, he broke it and said, 'This is my body that is for you. Do this in remembrance of me. In the same way he took the cup also, after supper, saying, 'This cup is the new covenant in my blood. Do this, as often as you drink it, in remembrance of me. For as often as you eat the bread and drink the cup, you proclaim the Lord's death until he comes."

Remember! The Greek word for "remembrance" is "anamnesis." The Hebrew word for remembrance is "zikkaron."

As in the celebration of the Jewish Passover, those who partake in the Lord's Supper, are involved in an event where God's saving action becomes present NOW!

Lord Jesus, you are truly the Lamb of God. Your are truly our Passover Lamb. We rejoice that we may receive your Body and Blood. We rejoice that your saving action on our behalf is happening right now. Thank you for the joy of proclaiming your triumph on the Cross. We await with joy your return in glory. Praise to you, Lord Jesus Christ.

Friday, April 18, 2014 Friday of the Lord's Passion, Good Friday
Hebrews 4, 14-16; 5, 7-9
Jesus, Compassionate High Priest

"Christ the victim, Christ the priest." These words from the Easter hymn, "At the Lamb's High Feast We Sing," came to mind as I prayed over today's reading.

Yes, it is Good Friday, but we know Easter will be here soon!

"Since, then we have a great high priest who has passed through the heavens, Jesus, the Son of God, let us hold fast to our confession. For we do not have a high priest who is unable to sympathize with our weaknesses, but we have one who in every respect has been tested as we are, yet without sin. Let us therefore approach the throne of grace with boldness, so that we may receive mercy and find grace to help in time of need (vv. 14-16)."

Boldness! The Greek word is "parrhesia." This boldness was noted in the life of St. Therese of Lisieux, the "Little Flower." She had a childlike, holy boldness in approaching God.

We too can be confident, bold, and even blunt when we approach God. God knows. God became human like us and understands us through and through.

Suffering. Jesus suffered and we will suffer as we follow him

"In the days of his flesh, Jesus offered up prayers and supplications, with loud cries and tears, to the one who was able to save him from death, and he was heard because of his reverent submission. Although he was a Son, he learned obedience through what he suffered; and having been made perfect, he became the source of eternal salvation for all who obey him… (vv. 7-9)."

Lord Jesus, you came from heaven to become human like us. You showed us what your Father in heaven is really like. You healed the sick, you raised the dead, and you cast out tormenting, unclean spirits. It was for us that you suffered. For us, you died. Once and for all, heal any distorted ideas we may have about your intentions of love towards us. Free us today, this GOOD Friday, to stand at your Cross to comfort you, to worship you, and to adore you. You are our King enthroned on a Cross. You are our King who will return in dazzling glory. Praise to you, Lord Jesus Christ.

> Saturday, April 19, 2014   The Easter Vigil of the Lord
> Genesis 22, 1-18
> The Testing of Abraham

Test! Abraham had been tested before.

Abraham had to keep on believing that what God had promised would indeed be fulfilled, even though it seemed wildly impossible. How could a 100 year old man with a barren 99 year old wife ever conceive a child?!

"Hoping against hope, he [Abraham] believed that he would become 'the father of many nations,' according to what was said, 'So numerous shall your descendants be.' He did not weaken in faith when he considered his own body, which was already as good as dead (for he was about a hundred years old). or when he considered the barrenness of Sarah's womb. No distrust made him waver concerning the promise of God, but he grew strong in his faith as he gave glory to God, being fully convinced that God was able to do what he had promised (Romans 4, 18-21)."

Test! Isaac was indeed born to Abraham and Sarah. Isaac, the promised son, was here. Now comes the really big test.

Would Abraham continue to trust God and to place God first? Would Abraham be willing to relinquish Isaac, his promised son, to God?

Abraham knew that obedience to God and worship of God took priority over every other aspect of his life. He even told his servants that he knew that God would provide (Genesis 22, 8).

Because of his determination to obey God at all cost and to relinquish even his beloved son Isaac to God, there was a dramatic intervention.

Blessing! The test was over, thanks be to God.

Because of Abraham's radical trust in the Lord, he was rewarded beyond comprehension. "I will indeed bless you, and I will make your offspring as numerous as the stars of heaven and as the sand that is on the seashore. And your offspring shall possess the gate of their enemies, and by your offspring shall all the nations of the earth gain blessing for themselves, because you have obeyed my voice (Genesis 22, 17-18)."

Lord Jesus, we entrust ourselves and those we hold dear into your loving care. Your love is beyond comprehension. You are worthy of our complete trust and our radical obedience. Thank you for the Holy Spirit who strengthens us to continue to trust you and to obey you. ALLELUIA!

Sunday, April 20, 2014
Easter Sunday of the Resurrection of the Lord
Colossians 3, 1-4
Mystical Death and Resurrection

Death. Christ's death on the Cross was not "mystical."

His death on the Cross was physical. He died. He died. He died.

Yes, but, as in the words of the Easter hymn, "Now the Green Blade Rises," we know that Our Lord has indeed been raised.

Resurrection! Christ's resurrection was not a "mystical" resurrection.

He rose from the dead. His body was resurrected. He truly rose from the dead.

In your Baptism, you died with Christ. "… when you were buried with him in baptism, you were also raised with him through faith in the power of God, who raised him from the dead (Colossians 2, 12)."

It is in our present life that you and I are risen with Christ. How are we to live?

"So if you have been raised with Christ, seek the things that are above, where Christ is, seated at the right hand of God. Set your minds on things that are above, not on things that are on earth, for you have died, and your life is hidden with Christ in God. When Christ who is your life is revealed, then you will also be revealed with him in glory (Colossians 3, 1-4)."

Let us read 1 Corinthians 15 and pray over it. The Holy Spirit will teach us many things about our life here on earth and our life when we experience the resurrection of our own earthly bodies.

Lord Jesus, you are the Lamb of God who was sacrificed for us. Let us keep your resurrection feast by living your resurrection life. ALLELUIA!

Sunday, April 27, 2014 Second Sunday of Easter
Divine Mercy Sunday
1 Peter 1, 3-9
Greeting; Blessing

We rejoice and continue to sing with all our hearts the glorious Easter hymn, "Jesus Christ is Risen Today."

"Blessed be the God and Father of our Lord Jesus Christ! By his great mercy he has given us a new birth into a living hope through the resurrection of Jesus Christ from the dead, and into an inheritance that is imperishable, undefiled, and unfading, kept in heaven for you ... (vv. 1-4)."

Rejoice! While on earth, we rejoice even in the midst of our trials.

"In this you rejoice, even if now for a little while you have had to suffer various trials, so that the genuineness of your faith – being more precious than gold that, though perishable, is tested by fire – may be found to result in praise and glory and honor when Jesus Christ is revealed) vv. 6-7)."

Our goal! Our goal, our true goal, is in sight.

The salvation of our souls! This is our true goal, not to be forgotten.

"Although you have not seen him, you love him; and even though you do not see him now, you believe in him and rejoice with an indescribable and glorious joy, for you are receiving the outcome of your faith, the salvation of your souls (v. 8)."

Lord Jesus, thank you for the Holy Spirit who reminds us daily of our true goal. The goal above all other goals. The salvation of our souls! What could be greater? Thank you for this time of intense purification in which we are being prepared to live in the glory of heaven for all eternity ALLELUIA!

Sunday, May 4, 2014 Third Sunday of Easter
1 Peter 1, 17-21
Reverence

Father! Our heavenly Father loves us. We are called to honor and to respect our Father.

"If you invoke as Father the one who judges all people impartially according to their deeds, live in reverent fear during the time of your exile (v. 17)."

Reverent! We are reverent, knowing that we have been ransomed by the Blood of Christ.

"You know that you were ransomed from the futile ways inherited from your ancestors, not with perishable things like silver or gold, but with the precious blood of Christ, like that of a lamb without defect or blemish (vv. 18-19)."

For us! Christ was revealed for US.

"He was destined before the foundation of the world, but was revealed at the end of the ages for your sake. Through him you have come to trust in God, who raised him from the dead and gave him glory, so that your faith and hope are set on God (vv. 19, 20)."

Lord Jesus, thank you for the Holy Spirit who reassures us of our Father's love for us. Let us respond with trust and reverence during this time of our sojourn on earth. Thank you for the place you are preparing for us in heaven, in the house of our Father. ALLELUIA!

Sunday, May 11, 2014 Fourth Sunday of Easter
1 Peter 2, 20b-25
Christ's Slaves

Suffering! "For to this you have been called, because Christ also suffered for you, leaving you an example, so that you should follow in his steps. 'He committed no sin, and no deceit was found in his mouth.' When he was abused, he did not return abuse; when he suffered, he did not threaten; but he entrusted himself to the one who judges justly (vv. 21-23)."

Freedom! Jesus " ... bore our sins in his body on the cross, so that, free from sins, we might live for righteousness ...(v. 24a)."

Healing! How amazing that "...by his wounds you have been healed. For you were going astray like sheep, but now you have returned to the shepherd and guardian of your souls (24b-25)."

Lord Jesus, you are our Good Shepherd. You are guarding our souls and keeping us safe for all eternity. Thank you for the Holy Spirit who is teaching us an eternal perspective as we continue our pilgrimage to live with you in the house of our Father. ALLELUIA!

Sunday, May 18, 2014 Fifth Sunday of Easter
1 Peter 2, 4-9
God's House and People

"Come to him [Jesus], a living stone, though rejected by mortals, yet chosen and precious in God's sight, and like living stones, let yourselves be built into a spiritual house, to be a holy priesthood, to offer spiritual sacrifices acceptable to God through Jesus Christ (vv. 4-5)."

Now comes the hard part of the discipleship package! Rejection. Misunderstanding. Suffering.

Jesus was the stone rejected. "To you then who believe, he is precious; but for those who do not believe, 'The stone that the builders rejected has become the very head of the corner (v. 7).'"

Jesus knew all forms of suffering. One of the most painful forms of suffering was the suffering of being misunderstood and rejected.

Remember the prologue to John's Gospel. "He was in the world, and the world came into being through him; yet the world did not know him. He came to what was his own, and his own people did not accept him (John 1, 10-11)."

Remember. You and I are called to remember our identity.

"But you are a chosen race, a royal priesthood, a holy nation, God's own people, in order that you may proclaim the mighty acts of him who called you out of darkness into his marvelous light (v. 9)."

If we truly follow Christ, we will share his suffering. There is no way around this.

"I want to know Christ and the power of his resurrection and the sharing of his sufferings by becoming like him in his death, if somehow I may attain the resurrection from the dead (Philippians 3, 10-11)."

Lord Jesus, you understood all about suffering and rejection. You were the stone rejected who became the cornerstone. Thank you for choosing us to be holy and to offer you sacrifices of praise and thanksgiving. Thank you for calling us to share in your Easter victory. ALLELUIA!

Sunday, May 25, 2014 Sixth Sunday of Easter
1 Peter 3, 15-18
Christian Suffering

DO NOT BE AFRAID!

"Now who will harm you if you are eager to do what is good? But even if you do suffer for doing what is right, you are blessed. Do not fear what they fear, and do not be intimidated, but in your hearts sanctify Christ as Lord. Always be ready to make your defense to anyone who demands from you an accounting for the hope that is in you; yet do it with gentleness and reverence. Keep your conscience clear, so that, when you are maligned, those who abuse you for your good conduct in Christ may be put to shame. For it is better to suffer for doing good, if suffering should be God's will, than to suffer for doing evil. For Christ also suffered for sins once for all, the righteous for the unrighteous, in order to bring you to God. He was put to death in the flesh, but made alive in the spirit ... (1 Peter 3, 13-18)."

We are called to sanctify Christ as Lord. We are not called to sanctify fear as Lord.

Sometimes, when we are afraid, we actually make an idol of fear and let fear rule our lives. This is not how we are called to live.

We are to sanctify CHRIST! We may indeed be afraid, but we know that Jesus is our Lord and that he holds the keys of victory for us.

Lord Jesus, thank you for the Holy Spirit who helps us to be gentle and reverent as we share our faith with others. Thank you for the gift of the sacrament of reconciliation as we seek to keep our conscience clear. You know how we shrink from suffering, and yet you suffered willingly for us. Thank you for the Holy Spirit who strengthens us to live for your glory. Alleluia!

Sunday, June 1, 2014 The Ascension of the Lord
Ephesians 1, 17-23
The Church as Christ's Body

Eyes! The eyes of the heart? Is this some kind of science fiction?

"I pray that the God of our Lord Jesus Christ, the Father of glory, may give you a spirit of wisdom and revelation as you come to know him, so that, with the eyes of your heart enlightened, you may know what is the hope to which he has called you, and what are the riches of his glorious inheritance among the saints, and what is the immeasurable greatness of his power for us who believe, according to the working of his great power. God put this power to work in Christ when he raised him from the dead and seated him at his right hand in the heavenly places, far above every name that is named, not only in this age but also in the age to come (vv. 17-21)."

All! Feet Head. Body.

"And he has put all things under his feet and has made him the head over all things for the church, which is his body, the fullness of him who fills all in all (Ephesians 1, 22 - 23)."

Lord Jesus, you are in charge! You are Head over all things concerning the Church. We are your Church, your Bride and your Body here on earth. Thank you for the Holy Spirit who opens the eyes of our hearts to the greatness of your call to us and enlarges our vision of your glory in the heavenly realm at the right hand of our Father. Let us now live lives which reflect your power and your glory within us. ALLELUIA!

Sunday, June 8, 2014 Pentecost Sunday
1 Corinthians 12, 3b-7, 12-13
Unity and Variety; One Body, Many Parts

JESUS IS LORD! "Now there are varieties of gifts, but the same Spirit, and there are varieties of services, but the same Lord, and there are varieties of activities, but it is the same God who activates all of them in everyone. To each is given the manifestation of the Spirit for the common good (vv. 4-7)."

JESUS IS LORD! "For just as the body is one and has many members, and all of the members of the body, though many, are one body, so it is with Christ. For in the one Spirit we were all baptized into one body … (vv. 12-13).

Lord Jesus, thank you for the Holy Spirit who teaches us that YOU are Lord and that we are all parts of your Body on earth, the Church. Let us learn to be confident as we live for your glory and travel to the house of our Father. ALLELUIA!

Sunday, June 15, 2014 The Most Holy Trinity
2 Corinthians 13, 11-13
Conclusion

The Holy Trinity!

I recently heard (on You Tube) the choir of Keble College in Oxford sing St. Patrick's "I Bind unto Myself Today the Strong Name of the Trinity." This majestic hymn transports us into the mystery of the Lord's incarnation, death, resurrection and then enfolds us into his breastplate ("Christ be with me, etc)."

St. Paul concludes his letter to the Christians in Corinth. He beseeches them to mend their unloving ways and to learn to get along with each other.

"Finally, brothers and sisters, farewell. Put things in order, listen to my appeal, agree with one another, live in peace; and the God of love and peace will be with you. Greet one another with a holy kiss. All the saints greet you. The grace of the Lord Jesus Christ, the love of God, and the communion of the Holy Spirit be with all of you."

Lord Jesus, we rejoice in your Easter victory! Thank you for the Holy Spirit who gives us the power to continue to follow you all the way Home to our Father's house. Alleluia!

Sunday, June 22, 2014 Corpus Christi
The Most Holy Body and Blood of Christ
1 Corinthians 10, 16-17
Warning against Idolatry

"The cup of blessing that we bless, is it not a sharing in the blood of Christ? The bread that we break, is it not a sharing in the body of Christ? Because there is one bread, we who are many are one body, for we all partake of the one bread."

"Therefore, my dear friends, flee from the worship of idols You cannot drink the cup of the Lord and the cup of demons. I do not want you to be partners with demons. You cannot drink the cup of the Lord and the cup of demons. You cannot partake of the table of the Lord and the table of demons (1 Corinthians 10, 14, 20b, 21)."

Lord Jesus, how can it be that we actually participate in your Body and Blood? Thank you for the Holy Spirit who teaches us that we are truly one Body. Thank you for giving your very Body and Blood to be our food for the journey Home to our Father in heaven. Alleluia!

Tuesday, June 24, 2014 The Nativity of St. John the Baptist
Acts. 13, 22-26
Paul's Address in the Synagogue

Herald! John the Baptist heralded the coming of Jesus, the Savior.

In Advent, with energy and expectation, we sing "On Jordan's Bank the Baptist's Cry." John was called to be the herald of our Lord.

The angel Gabriel had been sent from God to tell the elderly priest Zechariah that he and wife Elizabeth, also of priestly lineage, would become the parents of a son who was to be named John.

"He will turn many of the people of Israel to the Lord their God. With the spirit and power of Elijah he will go before him, to turn the hearts of parents to their children, and the disobedient to the wisdom of the righteous, to make ready a people prepared for the Lord (Luke 1, 16, 17)."

Called. Concealed. Revealed.

John had been carefully prepared for his vocation. He was called to point to Jesus as the Lamb of God. As a child, John " …grew and became strong in spirit, and he was in the wilderness until the day he appeared publicly to Israel (Luke 1, 80)."

Lord Jesus, thank you that you call us to follow you, you conceal us during our wilderness time when we are being purified and prepared for your service, and then, when you know that the time is right, you reveal us for the purpose for which we were created. Thank you for the Holy Spirit who strengthens us to wait with joyful patience. Alleluia!

Friday, June 27, 2014 Sacred Heart of Jesus
1 John 4, 7-16
God's Love and Christian Life

We sing Ralph Vaughn William's "Come Down O Love Divine" and pray to know how much the Lord truly loves us. There is a beautiful version of this from the choir of King's College, Cambridge, we may enjoy on You Tube.

Beloved! We are truly the beloved of God.

In this reading we are caught up into the mystery of the Holy Trinity. Father. Son Holy Spirit

A mystery of love. A mystery in which we are included.

"By this we know that we abide in him and he in us, because he has given us of his Spirit. And we have seen and do testify that the Father has sent his Son as the Savior of the world. God abides in those who confess that Jesus is the Son of God, and they abide in God. So we have known and believe the love that God has for us (vv. 13-16)."

Love springs forth from GOD! God loves us with a passion beyond our comprehension.

It may take us a while truly to believe. Truly to believe that God loves us.

We know God loves us, but it may take a lifetime to truly BELIEVE in this fathomless love.

Still, we long to believe. We believe and we begin to love one another.

"Beloved, let us love one another, because love is from God; everyone who loves is born of God and knows God (v. 7)."

God IS love. "No one has ever seen God; if we love one another, God lives in us, and his love is perfected in us (v. 12)."

"God's love was revealed among us in this way: God sent his only Son into the world so that we might live through him. In this is love, not that we loved God but that he loved us and sent his Son to be the atoning sacrifice for our sins. Beloved, since God loved us so much, we also ought to love one another (vv. 9-11)."

Lord Jesus, thank you for the Holy Spirit who breathes life and love into us and assures us of your love for us and of our Father's love for us. IT IS TRUE! Thank you for the Holy Spirit who strengthens us to love you, to love ourselves, to love others, and to stay in love. Alleluia!

Sunday, June 29, 2014 Saints Peter and Paul
2 Timothy 4, 6-8, 17
Reward for Fidelity; Paul's Loneliness

"In the presence of God and of Christ Jesus, who is to judge the living and the dead, and in view of his appearing and his kingdom, I solemnly urge you: proclaim the message; be persistent whether the time is favorable or unfavorable; convince, rebuke, and encourage, with the utmost patience in teaching. As for me, I am already being poured out as a libation, and the time of my departure has come. I have fought the good fight, I have finished the race, I have kept the faith. From now on there is reserved for me the crown of righteousness, which the Lord, the righteous judge, will give me on that day; and not only to me but also to all who have longed for his appearing. At my first defense no one came to my support, but all deserted me. May it not be counted against them! But the Lord stood by me and gave me strength, so that through me the message might be fully proclaimed and all the Gentiles might hear it. So I was rescued from the lion's mouth. The Lord will rescue me from every evil attack and save me for his heavenly kingdom. To him be the glory forever and ever. Amen (2 Timothy 4, 1-2, 6-8, 16-18)."

Poured out! That's what we see clearly at ordinations in the Roman Catholic Church.

Those to be ordained lie prostrate before the altar. They will be poured out as a most holy offering to the Lord for the purposes of the Lord.

Paul understood this very well. He was rapidly putting his life in review and in perspective.   Yes, there were those who had bitterly opposed him. Yes, there were those who sought to harm him and indeed to destroy him.

Did they succeed? No.

The Lord was with Paul and is with us. The Lord stood by Paul and is standing with us, right beside us.

Lord Jesus, thank you for choosing the weak and making them strong and mighty in bearing witness to you. You also choose those who think they are strong and you reveal to them their weakness and their need of complete dependence upon you. Thank you for the Holy Spirit who strengthens us to dwell on your word to us and to tend your flock. Alleluia!

Sunday, July 6, 2014 Fourteenth Sunday in Ordinary Time
Romans 8, 9, 11-13
The Flesh and the Spirit

"To set the mind on the flesh is death, but to set the mind on the Spirit is life and peace. For this reason the mind that is set on the flesh is hostile to God; it does not submit to God's law – indeed it cannot, and those who are in the flesh cannot please God. But you are not in the flesh; you are in the Spirit, since the Spirit of God dwells in you. Anyone who does not have the Spirit of Christ does not belong to him. But if Christ is in you, though the body is dead because of sin, the Spirit is life because of righteousness. If the Spirit of him who raised Jesus from the dead dwells in you, he who raised Christ from the dead will give life to your mortal bodies through his Spirit that dwells in you (Romans 8, 6-11)."

While still living in these bodies of flesh, these earthly bodies, we are also living in the realm of the Holy Spirit. God's Holy Spirit dwells within us. This is the same Holy Spirit who raised Jesus from the dead!

We don't have to live just any old way, according to the whims of our human nature. We don't have to do just any old thing we might be tempted to do.

We have a great power WITHIN us to purify us, to free us, and to strengthen us to live for GOD!

As Fr. John Foley's hymn reminds us, we are truly "Earthen Vessels." The powerful Holy Spirit is the treasure within our frail earthen vessels.

"So, then, brothers and sisters, we are debtors, not to the flesh, to live according to the flesh – for if you live according to the flesh, you will die; but if by the Spirit you put to death the deeds of the body, you will live (vv. 12-13)."

Lord Jesus, thank you for the powerful Holy Spirit who lives within us in an active way and who empowers us to glorify you while we are still on our pilgrimage to the heavenly Jerusalem, to the house of our Father. Alleluia!

Sunday, July 13, 2014 Fifteenth Sunday in Ordinary Time
Romans 8, 18-23
Destiny of Glory

Suffering. Glory. Creation.

"I consider that the sufferings of this present time are not worth comparing with the glory about to be revealed to us. For the creation waits with eager longing for the revealing of the children of God ... (vv. 18-19)."

Lord Jesus, thank you for the glimpses of glory you reveal to us as we suffer frustration and learn to wait to be revealed as God's children. Thank you for the Holy Spirit who strengthens us to follow you all the way through this present time of suffering and to enter, at last, into our true identity as your sisters and brothers. Alleluia!

Sunday, July 20, 2014 Sixteenth Sunday in Ordinary Time
Romans 8, 26-28
Destiny of Glory

The Holy Spirit " ... comes to the aid of our weakness; for we do not know how to pray as we ought, but the Spirit... intercedes with inexpressible groanings (v. 26)."

The Holy Spirit! The Holy Spirit intercedes for us with inexplicable intensity.

When we throw up our hands in despair and when our hearts sink with dismay, we are not left on our own. The Holy Spirit who lives within us is helping us, praying for us, and interceding for us. The Holy Spirit knows exactly what we need and knows exactly how to pray for us.

Lord Jesus, thank you for the Holy Spirit who intercedes for us according to the perfect plan of our Father in heaven. Alleluia!

Sunday, July 27, 2014 Seventeenth Sunday in Ordinary Time
Romans 8, 28-30
God's Indomitable Love in Christ

"We know that all things work together for good for those who love God, who are called according to his purpose. For those whom he foreknew he also predestined to be conformed to the image of his Son, in order that he might be the firstborn within a large family. And those whom he predestined he also called; and those whom he called he also justified; and those whom he justified he also glorified."

Lord Jesus, you knew all about us when you called us to come to you and to follow you. You called us for your own particular purpose. Thank you for the Holy Spirit who is justifying us and carefully molding us into your image. Thank you for the time when we will see you in all your glory and live forever with you in the house of our Father in heaven. Alleluia

Sunday, August 3, 2014 Eighteenth Sunday in Ordinary Time
Romans 8, 35, 37-39
God's Indomitable Love in Christ

"Who will separate us from the love of Christ? Will hardship, or distress, or persecution, or famine, or nakedness, or peril, or sword? No, in all these things we are more than conquerors through him who loved us. For I am convinced that neither death, nor life, nor angels, nor rulers, nor things present, nor things to come, nor powers, nor height, nor depth, nor anything else in all creation, will be able to separate us from the love of God in Christ Jesus our Lord."

We conquer! Even when we are in the deepest distress and suffering, we conquer. We are mighty conquerors through the unfathomable love of God in Christ.

Lord Jesus, sometimes we feel so overwhelmed by our own sins and suffering and by the sins and suffering of others. We feel stifled and can hardly breathe. Thank you for the Holy Spirit who breathes new life and hope into us. to continue to trust you and to follow you all the way Home to our Father in heaven. Alleluia!

Wednesday, August 6, 2014 The Transfiguration of the Lord
2 Peter 1, 16-19
Apostolic Witness

Peter! Peter was there. Peter recalled his experience of being one of the eye-witnesses of the dazzling transfiguration of Jesus.

"For we did not follow cleverly devised myths when we made known to you the power and coming of our Lord Jesus Christ, but we had been eyewitnesses of his majesty. For he received honor and glory from God the Father when that voice was conveyed to him by the Majestic Glory, saying, 'This is my Son, my Beloved, with whom I am well pleased.' We ourselves heard this voice from heaven, while we were with him on the holy mountain. So we have the prophetic message more fully confirmed. You will do well to be attentive to this as to a lamp shining in a dark place, until the day dawns and the morning star rises in your hearts."

Identity! From the clouds of heaven came the voice of God the Father. "This is my Son, my Beloved (v. 17b)."

Identity! Jesus knew who he was.

Identity! Who are we? "For all who are led by the Spirit of God are children of God (Romans 8, 14)."

As God's children, how do we live? "For once you were darkness, but now in the Lord you are light. Live as children of light – for the fruit of light is found in all that is good and right and true (Ephesians 5, 8, 9)."

Lord Jesus, thank you for the Holy Spirit who reminds us to be attentive to you and to remember our identity as God's children. We are your sisters and brothers! Let us live bravely for your glory. Alleluia!

Sunday, August 10, 2014 Nineteenth Sunday in Ordinary Time
Romans 9, 1-5
Paul's Love for Israel

"I am speaking the truth in Christ.—I am not lying; my conscience confirms it by the Holy Spirit—I have great sorrow and unceasing anguish in my heart. For I could wish that I myself were accursed and cut off from Christ for the sake of my own people, and my kindred according to the flesh. They are Israelites, and to them belong the adoption, the glory, and the covenants, the giving of the law, the worship, and the promises; to them belong the patriarchs, and from them, according to the flesh, comes the Messiah, who is over all, God blessed forever. Amen."

The Israelites are God's own people. From the Israelites came Jesus, our Lord and Savior.

We long for the time when we will be one flock with one Shepherd. We long for the Wedding Supper of the Lamb.

Lord Jesus, thank you that you are our Good Shepherd and that you are leading us Home to our Father. Alleluia!

Friday, August 15, 2014 The Assumption of Mary
1 Corinthians 15, 20-27
Christ the First fruits

"If for this life only we have hoped in Christ, we are of all people most to be pitied. But in fact Christ has been raised from the dead, the first fruits of those who have died. For since death came through a human being, the resurrection of the dead has also come through a human being; for as all die in Adam, so all will be made alive in Christ. But each in his own order: Christ the first fruits, then at his coming those who belong to Christ. Then comes the end, when he hands over the kingdom to God the Father, after he has destroyed every ruler and every authority and power. For he must reign until he has put all his enemies under his feet. The last enemy to be destroyed is death (1 Corinthians 15, 19-27)."

Lord Jesus, thank you for the choice your Mother Mary made to say yes. She said yes to God. Thank you for the Holy Spirit who strengthens us to say yes to all that you require of us as we follow you Home to the house of our Father. Alleluia!

Sunday, August 17, 2014 Twentieth Sunday in Ordinary Time
Romans 11, 13-15, 29-32
The Gentiles' Salvation; God's Irrevocable Call

"Now I am speaking to you Gentiles. Inasmuch then as I am an apostle to the Gentiles, I glorify my ministry in order to make my own [Jewish] people jealous, and thus save some of them. For if their rejection is the reconciliation of the world, what their acceptance be but life from the dead (vv. 13-15)."

God's call cannot be revoked … "for the gifts and the calling of God are irrevocable (v. 29)."

God's call cannot be revoked. God's mercy triumphs!

God's calling defies all human logic. "… God chose what is foolish in the world to shame the wise; God chose what is weak in the world to shame the strong; God chose what is low and despised in the world, things that are not, to reduce to nothing things that are, so that no one might boast in the presence of God (1 Corinthians 1, 27-29)."

The English poet and clergyman, George Herbert (1593-1633) wrote <u>A Priest to the Temple: or the Country Parson</u>, his famous prose work. The collection of his poems is called <u>The Temple</u>. An especially beautiful poem, "The Call," has been set to music by Ralph Vaughn Williams. You may hear this sung in St. Peter's Catholic Church in Columbia, South Carolina (You Tube).

Lord Jesus, thank you for calling us, Jew and Gentile, to follow you. Thank you for pouring out your unfathomable mercy upon us. We praise you and give you all the glory. Alleluia!

Sunday, August 24, 2014 Twenty-first Sunday in Ordinary Time
Romans 11, 33-36
Triumph of God's Mercy

"O the depths of the riches and wisdom and knowledge of God! How unsearchable are his judgments and how inscrutable his ways! 'For who has known the mind of the Lord? Or who has been his counselor?' 'Or who has given a gift to him, to receive a gift in return?' For from him and through him and to him are all things. To him be the glory forever. Amen."

Lord Jesus, with the angels we sing your praise. You continue to choose the weak and frail and, in your mysterious mercy, you make them strong and mighty in bearing witness to you. Glory to you, our Lord and our God. Alleluia!

Sunday, August 31, 2014 Twenty-second Sunday in Ordinary Time
Romans 12, 1-2
Sacrifice of Body and Mind

"I appeal to you therefore, brothers and sisters, by the mercies of God, to present your bodies as a living sacrifice, holy and acceptable to God, which is your spiritual worship. Do not be conformed to this world, but be transformed by the renewing of your minds, so that you may discern what is the will of God—what is good and acceptable and perfect."

Image. We are not called to worry about our image in this world.

We are not to be conformed to this world. We are called to be molded into the image of Christ (Romans 8, 29). This is the work of the Holy Spirit.

Lord Jesus, with all our hearts we offer ourselves to you – body, soul, and spirit. We are living sacrifices ready for use in your kingdom.

Thank you for the Holy Spirit who is renewing us and transforming us into your image. Thank you that your plan for us is perfect. We place all our trust in you. Alleluia!

> Sunday, September 7, 2014
> Twenty-third Sunday in Ordinary Time
> Romans 13, 8-10
> Love Fulfills the Law

"Owe no one anything, except to love one another; for the one who loves another has fulfilled the law. The commandments, 'You shall not commit adultery; You shall not murder; You shall not steal; You shall not covet'; and any other commandment, are summed up in this word, 'Love your neighbor as yourself.' Love does no wrong to a neighbor; therefore, love is the fulfilling of the law."

Lord Jesus, thank you for the Holy Spirit who strengthens us to love others as you love us. Alleluia!

> Sunday, September 14, 2014 Exaltation of the Holy Cross
> Philippians 2, 6-11
> Plea for Unity and Humility

Jesus! He was already "there."

He was in heaven. He was in the form of God.

And yet, for us he came down from heaven. We were like scruffy lost sheep and lambs, helplessly starving in the wilderness.

As Pope Benedict XVI said, "The Son of God will not let this happen; he cannot abandon humanity in so wretched a condition. He leaps to his feet and abandons the glory of heaven, in order to go in search of the sheep and pursue it, all the way to the Cross. He takes it upon his shoulders and carries our humanity; he carries us all—he is the good shepherd who lays down his life for the sheep (Pope Benedict XVI, Inaugural Homily, April 24, 2005, St. Peter's Square)."

For us he lived. For us he died. For us, he returned, mission accomplished, to the glory of heaven, where he is preparing a place for us.

Radical! Because of Jesus' radical humility, he, the holy Lamb of God, offered himself on the Cross in order to have us with him in heaven for all eternity.

Therefore, God the Father has highly exalted him and given him the Name that is above every other name. The Name of Jesus will cause every knee to bow. The Name of Jesus will cause every tongue to acknowledge that JESUS CHRIST IS LORD!

We rejoice today! With joy and thanksgiving, we sing "Lift High the Cross."

Lord Jesus, you have already won the victory for us. We are secure in you and in your love and care for us. Thank you for the Holy Spirit who is strengthening us to be brave as we live for you in this world which rages against you and your love. Let us continue to follow you all the way Home. Glory! Alleluia!

Sunday, September 21, 2014
Twenty-fifth Sunday in Ordinary Time
Philippians 1, 20-24, 27
Progress of the Gospel; Steadfastness in Faith

"It is my eager expectation and hope that I will not be put to shame in any way, but that by my speaking with all boldness, Christ will be exalted now as always in my body, whether by life or by death. For to me, living is Christ and dying is gain (vv. 20-21)."

Once, after a time of illness, I wondered how Christ could be magnified in my life. How could this exhaustion of body, soul, and spirit glorify Christ? It was necessary to remind myself that to live is CHRIST!

How do we live? St. Paul reminds us, "Only, live your life in a manner worthy of the gospel of Christ … (v. 27a)."

Lord Jesus, thank you for the Holy Spirit who strengthens us to continue to follow you. Thank you for the Holy Spirit who instructs us how to conduct ourselves in a way that is worthy of your Gospel. We yield to your plan for us and we choose to honor you with our trust and our obedience. Thank you for the joy of seeing you face to face in the house of our Father. Alleluia!

Sunday, September 28, 2014
Twenty-sixth Sunday in Ordinary Time
Philippians 2, 1-11
Plea for Unity and Humility

"Do nothing from selfish ambition or conceit, but in humility regard others as better than yourselves (v. 3).

OUCH!!! How can we get by without healthy ambition, a lot of cheap bragging, name-dropping, and fluffing up our C.V.? Oh, and all the while, keeping our holy demeanor intact?

St. Paul says to regard others as BETTER than ourselves. SCREAM! But what if we think we ARE better than "they" are?

Humility! Here is the key.

If we have the humility to believe, really believe, that others are more important than we are, we will have no problem refraining boasting and from selfishness. "Let each of you look not to your own interests, but to the interests of others (v. 4)."

"Let this same mind be in you that was in Christ Jesus, who, though he was in the form of God, did not regard equality with God as something to be exploited, but emptied himself, taking the form of a slave, being born in human likeness. And being found in human form, he humbled himself and became obedient to the point of death –even death on a cross (vv. 5-8)."

Jesus, the Son of God, came to us as a slave. He came to serve.

"Therefore God also highly exalted him and gave him the name that is above every name, that at the name of Jesus every knee shall bend, in heaven and on earth and under the earth, and every tongue confess that Jesus Christ is Lord, to the glory of God the Father (vv. 9-11)."

The name. The name of JESUS!

"At the Name of Jesus." I love this hymn written by Caroline Maria Noel (1817-1877). It has been set to music both by Ralph Vaughn Williams (1872-1958) and by Christopher Walker, a very gifted contemporary English composer.

Lord Jesus, we stand in awe of your majestic humility? How could you go through all that for us? Forgive us for trying to vindicate ourselves and trying to promote ourselves. Have mercy on us. YOU and you alone are the desire of our heart. We live to glorify YOU. Alleluia!

Sunday, October 5, 2014
Twenty-seventh Sunday in Ordinary Time
Philippians 4, 6-9
Joy and Peace

"Rejoice in the Lord always; again I will say, Rejoice. Let your gentleness be known by everyone. The Lord is near. Do not worry about anything, but in everything by prayer and supplication with thanksgiving let your requests be made known to God. And the peace of God, which surpasses all understanding, will guard your hearts and your minds in Christ Jesus. Finally, beloved, whatever is true, whatever is pure, whatever is pleasing, whatever is commendable, if there is any excellence and if there is anything worthy of praise, think about these things. Keep on doing the things that you have learned and received and heard and seen in me, and the God of peace will be with you (Philippians 4, 4-9)."

Keep on! In the midst of our exhaustion, our trials, our joys, and our suffering, we are called to keep living for Jesus. The God of all peace and comfort is with us.

"Deliver us, Lord, from every evil, and grant us peace in our day. In your mercy keep us free from sin and protect us from all anxiety as we wait in joyful hope for the coming of our Savior Jesus Christ (the Libere nos from the 1973 Sacramentary, p. 562)."

Lord Jesus, thank you for the Holy Spirit who strengthens us to keep on. Alleluia!

Sunday, October 12, 2014
Twenty-eighth Sunday in Ordinary Time
Philippians 4, 12-14, 19-20
Gratitude for the Philippians' Generosity

"I know what it is to have little, and I know what it is to have plenty. In any and all circumstances I have learned the secret of being well-fed and of going hungry, of having plenty and of being in need. I can do all things through him who strengthens me (vv. 12-13)."

Paul knew that his strength came from the Lord. Therefore he could reassure the Philippians of the Lord's provision for them.

"And my God will fully satisfy every need of yours according to his riches in glory in Christ Jesus. To our God and Father be glory forever and ever. Amen (vv. 19-20)."

Lord Jesus, thank you for the Holy Spirit who strengthens me to do what you have called me to do. Alleluia!

Sunday, October 19, 2014
Twenty-ninth Sunday in Ordinary Time
1 Thessalonians 1, 1-5
Thanksgiving for their Faith

Power! It is by the power of the Holy Spirit that the Gospel is proclaimed.

Power! It is by the power of the Holy Spirit that the Gospel is received.

Power! It is by the power of the Holy Spirit that the Gospel is lived.

Lord Jesus, thank you for the Holy Spirit who energizes us and strengthens us to BELIEVE you and to live for your glory. Alleluia!

Sunday, October 26, 2014 Thirtieth Sunday in Ordinary Time
1 Thessalonians 1, 5-10
Thanksgiving for Their Faith

Turning! The Christians in the city of Thessalonica, capital of the Roman province of Macedonia, turned from idolatry to the LIVING God! Paul, Sylvanus, and Timothy proclaimed the Gospel to them both in word and in action.

Suffering! The Thessalonians received the Gospel in a time of great persecution and suffering.

Joy! There was also the joy of the powerful Holy Spirit.

Lord Jesus, thank you for the Holy Spirit who strengthens us to continue turning from any "idols" in our lives and turn to the living GOD. Thank you for the Holy Spirit who is purifying us and preparing us for your return in glory. Alleluia!

Saturday, November 1, 2014 All Saints
1 John 3, 1-3
Children of God

As we sing with joy "For All the Saints," we remember who we are. We are indeed God's beloved children.

"See what love the Father has given us, that we should be called children of God; and that is what we are. The reason the world does not know us is that it did not know him. Beloved, we are God's children now; what we will be has not yet been revealed. What we do know is this: when he is revealed, we will be like him, for we will see him as he is. And all who have this hope in him purify themselves, just as he is pure."

Now! We are God's children right now.

That's exciting enough. But, wait, there's more to come! It has not yet been revealed to us what we shall become.

Lord Jesus, thank you for the Holy Spirit who is purifying us and preparing us for our glorious future. Alleluia!

Sunday, November 2, 2014 All Souls
The Commemoration of All the Faithful Departed
Romans 6, 3-9
Freedom from Sin; Life in God

Baptism. Death. Resurrection!

When we were baptized in water in the name of the Father, the Son, and the Holy Spirit, we were baptized into the death of our Lord Jesus Christ.

"Do you not know that all of us who have been baptized into Christ Jesus were baptized into his death? Therefore we have been buried with him by baptism into death, so that just as Christ was raised from the dead by the glory of the Father, so we too might walk in newness of life. For if we have been united with him in a death like his, we will certainly be united with him in a resurrection like his. We know that our old self was crucified with him so that the body of sin might be destroyed, and we might no longer be enslaved to sin. For whoever has died is freed from sin. But if we have died with Christ, we believe that we will also live with him. We know that Christ, being raised from the dead, will never die again; death no longer has dominion over him."

Lord Jesus, thank you that the Holy Spirit who raised you from the dead now dwells in us and is giving us the power to live for you. Alleluia!

Sunday, November 9, 2014
Dedication of the Lateran Basilica in Rome
1 Corinthians 3, 9c-11, 16-17
The Role of God's Ministers

"Do you not know that you are God's temple and that God's Spirit dwells in you? If anyone destroys God's temple, God will destroy that person. For God's temple is holy, and you are that temple (vv. 16-17).

Remember the hymn "Christ is Made the Sure Foundation." The stone rejected, he is both the head of the Church and the cornerstone.

Our Lord Jesus Christ is our foundation, our sure foundation. "For no one can lay any foundation other than the one that has been laid; that foundation is Jesus Christ (v. 11)."

Lord Jesus, thank you that you are our foundation. Thank you that we are God's temple and that the Holy Spirit is dwelling within us. Alleluia!

Sunday, November 16, 2014
Thirty-third Sunday in Ordinary Time
1 Thessalonians 5, 1-6
Vigilance

When I was an undergraduate political science major, one of my professors asked me, "Have you read <u>The Children of Light and The Children of Darkness</u>?"

Puzzling. I am still not sure why I was asked that question. The phrase "children of light," stayed with me.

Light! Jesus said, "You are the light of the world (Matthew 5, 13a)."

How do we then live out our call to be children of the light? St. Paul offers the following counsel.

"But we appeal to you, brother and sisters, to respect those who labor among you, and have charge of you in the Lord and admonish you; esteem them very highly in love because of their work. Be at peace among yourselves. And we urge you, beloved to admonish the idlers, encourage the fainthearted, help the weak, be patient with all of them. See that none of you repays evil for evil, but always seek to do good to one another and to all. Rejoice always, pray without ceasing, give thanks in all circumstances; for this is the will of God in Christ Jesus for you. Do not quench the Spirit. Do not despise the words of prophets, but test everything; hold fast to what is good, abstain from every form of evil. May the God of peace himself sanctify you entirely, and may your spirit and soul and body be kept sound and blameless at the coming of our Lord Jesus Christ. The one who calls you is faithful, and he will do this (1 Thessalonians 12-24)."

Lord Jesus, thank you for the Holy Spirit who is purifying us and strengthening us to live as children of the light as we await your return in glory. Alleluia!

>Sunday, November 23, 2014
>Our Lord Jesus Christ, King of the Universe
>1 Corinthians 15, 20-26, 28
>Christ the First fruits

"If for this life only we have hoped in Christ, we are of all people are most to be pitied. But in fact Christ has been raised from the dead, the first fruits of those who have died. For since death came through a human being, the resurrection of the dead has also come through a human being; for as all die in Adam, so all will be made alive in Christ. But each in his own order: Christ the first fruits, then at his coming those who belong to Christ. Then comes the end when he hands over the kingdom to God the Father, after he has destroyed every ruler and every authority and power. For he must reign until he has put all his enemies under his feet. The last enemy to be destroyed is death. When all things are subjected to him, then the Son himself will also be subjected to the one who put all things in subjection under him, so that God may be all in all (vv. 19 - 26, 28)."

What a glorious passage with which to wrap up the Church year. Christ the King! Christ the King of the universe. Indeed, we sing "The King of Glory Comes!"

Lord Jesus, you are Lord indeed. You are our King. You are King of all creation. Let us rejoice in your sovereignty over us and over all as we await your triumphant return in glory. Alleluia!

>Thursday, November 27, 2014 Thanksgiving Day
>1 Corinthians 1, 3-9
>Greeting; Thanksgiving

"Grace to you and peace from God our Father and the Lord Jesus Christ. I give thanks to my God always for you because of the grace of God that has been given you in Christ Jesus, for in every way you have been enriched in him, in speech and knowledge of every kind – just as the testimony of Christ has been strengthened among you – so that you are not lacking in any spiritual gift as you wait for the revealing of our Lord Jesus Christ. He will also strengthen you to the end, so that you may be blameless on the day of our Lord Jesus Christ. God is faithful; by him you were called into the fellowship of his Son, Jesus Christ our Lord."

What a relief! It is not all up to us.

"May the God of peace himself sanctify you entirely; and may your spirit and soul and body be kept sound and blameless at the coming of our Lord Jesus Christ. The one who calls you is faithful and he will do this (1 Thessalonians 5, 23-24)."

"I know that my Redeemer lives, and that at the last he will stand upon the earth; and after my skin has been thus destroyed, then in my flesh I shall see God, who I shall see on my side, and my eyes shall behold … (Job 19, 25-27a)."

Lord Jesus, thank you that you are faithful and true. Thank you for the Holy Spirit who is leading us each day closer to the house of our Father in heaven. Alleluia!

About the author

Janis Walker is the author of <u>Alleluia a Gospel Diary</u> and several other books. She studied New Testament Greek at Fuller Theological Seminary, received a Master's degree in Theology at St. Patrick's Seminary and also studied at the Graduate Theological Union in Berkeley. She has served in hospital ministry, retreat ministry, parish ministry and ecumenical prayer group ministry. On May 13, 1998, Janis was received into the Roman Catholic Church in Rossi Chapel at the Jesuit Retreat Center in a Chrism Mass for Christian Unity. She and her family live in California. Janis has a continuing interest in the ecclesial effects of the Oxford Movement and the legacy of Cardinal Newman.

A.M.D.G.

You may order additional copies of this book

from www.amazon.com, www.barnesandnoble.com,

or through your favorite bookstore.

www.ingramcontent.com/pod-product-compliance
Lightning Source LLC
Chambersburg PA
CBHW020004050426
42450CB00005B/311